Passing Your Heritage On

A Guide to Writing
Your Ethical Wills

Sharon Foltz, EdD

Copyright © 2007 by Sharon Foltz

ISBN 0-7414-3795-3

Published by Rainbow Ridge Publications,
19818 150th Ave. Indianola IA 50125.

This is a companion book to *Passing Your Heritage On: A Guide to Writing Your Family Stories*, available in bookstores and online.

If you would like information about quantity discounts, write to Dr. Foltz:

Write With You
Sharon Foltz, EdD
19818 150th Ave.
Indianola IA 50125-8658

e-mail foltz@iowatelecom.net

websites: http://www.writewithyou.com

http://www.ethicalwillexamples.com

Printed by:

INFI∞ITY
PUBLISHING.COM

1094 New DeHaven Street, Suite 100
West Conshohocken, PA 19428-2713
Info@buybooksontheweb.com
www.buybooksontheweb.com
Toll-free (877) BUY BOOK
Local Phone (610) 941-9999
Fax (610) 941-9959

Printed in the United States of America
Printed on Recycled Paper
Published June 2007

Table of Contents

Mission Statement

The mission of the writing consultant business *Write With You* is to assist individuals in writing the experiences and impressions from their own lifetime as well as the stories that have been passed down through their families during the passage of time and generations. *Write With You* intends not to write *for* the clients, but *with* them to preserve the storytellers' own voices. It is intended that each client gain the confidence to write further stories or perhaps personal communications in the form of letters to a specific child or grandchild, old friend, spouse, even an estranged relative. However, *Write With You* is most willing to continue to help if the client is more comfortable with assistance. The offer of assistance in creating ethical wills adds a new dimension to the possibilities of working together.

Acknowledgments

I have loved the concept of personal legacy — letters or letters of my heritage that had been written just for me for as long as I have been reading and writing. I have received exactly none. Well, I can twist the definition just a little and call the following an ethical will:

> **Colo Iowa Jan 20—1953**
>
> **Dear Sharon, this card is to let you know I am thinking of you and all the rest but this card is for you mostly because I Love You. it is a dark day, Ground covered with snow. be a good Girl to Those Brothers of yours. I will have to stop and go mail this. Write to me some day.**
>
> **Good Bye Love to all as ever your Grandfather**

My thoughts and thanks turn to my granddad's note. I had just turned eight years old and this was one of the first pieces of mail ever that had been sent just to me. The message is clear and smooth. It doesn't get snagged on the lack of punctuation or the repetitions.

My grandpa was born in 1877, so he was 75 years old, still living alone in his own house fifty miles from us. I was impressed that he would take the time to write to me and then take his painfully arthritic walk downtown to mail the letter. It means even more to me now to have the note to read.

Is that an ethical will? It barely qualifies, but it serves a small purpose and I enjoy it. I hadn't heard the term "ethical will" until I attended a conference of the Association of Personal Historians in 2003 and met Dr. Barry Baines. Practicing in Minneapolis, he holds several positions. One is Associate Director of a hospice. He is rapidly becoming the authority on ethical wills, and he seems to be pioneering a specialty of helping people write last-opportunity ethical wills from their hospice beds.

In this book I quote Dr. Baines broadly and often, because I see no point in reinventing the wheel. He has given us current definitions and uses in his fine book, *Ethical Wills: Putting your values on paper.* (Perseus Publishing, 2002) Reviewing the book, Lara Winner says, "*Ethical Wills* distills the best of Barry Baines' experience as a hospice physician and ethical will workshop leader and facilitator. ...(His)... goal is to promote the writing and use of the ethical will itself, to try to ensure that the most important words between family and friends do not remain unsaid. Who can argue with that?" Let's give him grateful credit and move on. Thank you, Barry.

In writing this book, I am attempting to present examples of a greater variety of ethical wills and a relaxed attitude to encourage the average Americans. If they see that I value a scrap of paper from my uneducated grandfather, (isn't it sad that I don't know for sure that he graduated from high school?) perhaps they will take the opportunity to leave a gift of love and dreams and history to their children and grandchildren. Rabbi Amy Ellberg tells the writers with whom she works that "writing an ethical will does not require enormous learning or wisdom. Whether it matches the great truths or not doesn't matter. It's what you have to give. What else can we give our children but who we are?" (Schulman)

My thanks to my parents, both of whom enjoyed their family histories, for their stories and their encouragement. I was able to help my mother by typing her memories of a midwestern farm childhood as she dictated. It made a charming booklet. My father retired, bought a word processor, then a computer, and was "getting organized" when he passed on. We kids inherited stories, charts, pictures, diplomas, licenses, advertising gimmicks, and books. We are grateful for the collection, but, if only there had been some form of a completed ethical will…

My brothers and I will finish our version of his memoirs, but it cannot be the same.

My gratitude to my family for their patience and encouragement. And for providing some of the very dreams and loving relationships that I must mention in my own ethical wills. I am in the preparation stages for most of them, but bits and pieces are being written as I make up examples for this book. There may a smidgin of truth in some of my examples. I am doing a great deal of thinking before I begin my own memoirs and ethical will letters, because I know that, for most of my loved ones, I won't be able to stop with just one letter.

About the Author

Who am I and why would I feel that I could inspire you to write and to improve your writing? I have the time now that I have retired from college teaching. Years ago I taught in elementary school until I married and resigned to rear three boys. After nearly twenty years, I went back to Drake University, in Des Moines, IA, teaching there to pay tuition and earning a Specialist in Education degree. I continued until I was awarded my Doctorate in Education.

For a few years I taught part time in ESL (English as a Second Language), Composition I and II (writing classes), and Reading and Study Skills in several small colleges.

I have helped students, from third-graders to college students, learn to write with clarity and interest. I don't claim technical expertise, but I feel this guide to writing ethical wills could help students of any age gain writing skills and confidence as they write their thoughts to their survivors and their future generations.

S.F.

Introduction

If you could do something for the good of your whole family, would you attempt it? If it weren't too costly or hard to do? And if someone were willing to help you every step of the way? What is this great but simple activity that you can do and how will it be so effective?

You can make your *ethical will*. I was tempted to name this book *From Letters to Libraries*. As that title would indicate, your ethical will can be one short letter or it can be several volumes, practically a library on its own. An ethical will can be created in an alternate form. It doesn't have to be written. There will be ideas and examples of different forms in this book. Whatever form you choose to employ, there are several ways that it becomes important to your loved ones after you have gone on.

There are many reasons to write your own ethical will, but in relation to your family members, the following ideas stand out as emotionally valuable.

1) Your ethical will can give great comfort and pleasure to your family. The loss your children and grandchildren

and even great-grandchildren feel immediately after your demise may be difficult for them. Think how comforted they could be through the subsequent years by reading or hearing your thoughts, your advice, your memories, your moral convictions, and perhaps your sense of humor. There is nothing that cannot be included in your ethical will if you want to write it. We will discuss later what items or subjects seem appropriate and which should be handled carefully, but it is your project, after all. You will be leaving something to tell people who you are and who you were.

2) It can establish in younger children a sense of belonging because they will realize that you took the time and made the effort to leave them some of your own thoughts. They may come to believe that they are an important part of your family. They may come to see themselves as one link of a chain extending back for generations and that they may forge a link to extend forward for an unknown number of generations.

3) An ethical will can pass on your heritage of ethics and moral convictions. You will be able to express your desire to give the next generations a guide to living and to explain how and why your concepts of ethics have served you well.

"Legal wills bequeath
your valuables.
Ethical wills bequeath
your values."

(Baines, 2002)

Chapter One

What is an Ethical Will?

One popular definition of the Ethical Will:

The ethical will is a way to share our values, blessings, life's lessons, hopes and dreams for the future, love, and forgiveness with your family, friends, and community. (Baines, 2002)

It is, in a sense, the way you can hand down your heritage of ethics and morals. If you feel strongly about how a life should be lived, you will want to leave those ideas and rules to those who follow you in life, those people who matter most to you and who have looked to you for guidance. You are able to offer your advice on handling the morality questions that we all face these days. A set of strong ethics can counter a great deal of temptation and confusion for those who read your thoughts on similar situations. Then they are able to apply the principles.

Before we go deeply into ethical wills, it might be helpful to determine what an ethical will is not. Most people are aware of the legal will and many people

1

have written one to indicate to their survivors how they would like to have their possessions and assets distributed after their death. The ethical will is not a substitute for your legal will and testament. It is not meant to replace your living will.

There are three basic types of wills used today:

1. A legal will is usually read after the death of the individual who made the will. It is a legal requirement that it be followed to the letter in order to fulfill the wishes of the individual as to the dispersal of his or her worldly goods.

2. A living will is to be read and followed while the author is still alive but has become unable to communicate his or her wishes regarding medical care, residence, or other critical information.

3. An ethical will can, and in most cases should, be read before the death of the author. Once, ethical wills were left to be read after the writer's death. Today, they are often read while the author is still able to explain his or her feelings and answer questions about the ethical will. The ethical will can also contain directions as to what the writer prefers for medical care and/or funeral arrangements.

To sum it up, a good ethical will explains the family

history, the life lessons the writer learned, experiences that contributed to his/her sense of values, and the application of those values to life situations. The ethical will can be passed on while the writer is able to explain or it can be put away in a safe but accessible place to be read after the writer's death. It doesn't give away the material goods, but passes on the non-material traditions and ethical values of the writer.

An Ancient Tradition

From the Bible (KJV), Gen. 9:15-16, we read an early promise from God to his people:

> I will remember my covenant which is between me and you and every living creature of all flesh; and the waters shall no more become a flood to destroy all flesh. And the (rain)bow shall be in the cloud and I will look upon it, that I may remember the everlasting covenant..,

And referring to advice handed down through an ethical will, we could say that the ultimate advice was given to Moses. In Deut. 9:11, Moses said:

> "And it came to pass at the end of forty days and forty nights, that the Lord gave me the two tables of stone, even the tables of the covenant."

Those tables of stone conveyed the Ten Commandments!

It is touching that Jacob spoke to each of his twelve

sons in Gen. 49:1-30. He praised their good qualities and was not reluctant to mention their shortcomings. The verses devoted to Joseph are filled with a father's pride and gratitude. Finally, he instructed the sons just how and where he wished to be buried.

Pharaoh respected Jacob's ethical will. He allowed Joseph to fulfill his father's wishes for burial. "And Joseph returned into Egypt, he, and his brethren, and all that went up with him to bury his father, after he had buried his father."

But the influence of Jacob's ethical will didn't end there. The brothers were frightened by the potential repercussions of their meanness to Joseph:

> And when Joseph's brethren saw that their father was dead, they said, Joseph will peradventure hate us, and will certainly requite us all the evil which we did unto him. And they sent a messenger unto Joseph, saying, Thy father did command before he died, saying, So shall ye say unto Joseph, Forgive, I pray thee now, the trespass of thy brethren, and their sin; for they did unto thee evil: and now, we pray thee, forgive the trespass of the servants of the God of Thy father, and Joseph wept when they spake unto him.

Jacob's traditional advice and instructions, handed down as part of his sons' heritage, blessed them all in the final outcome. The request that they forgive one another is a beautiful gesture and fulfilled one of

Jacob's hopes for the family.

Today's ethical will writer who offers advice and rules for life behavior is not so different from the speaker/writer of Proverbs 4:10-14:

> Hear, O my son, and receive my sayings; and the years of thy life shall be many. I have taught thee in the way of wisdom; I have led thee in right paths. When thou goest, thy steps shall not be straightened; and when thou runnest, thou shalt not stumble. Take fast hold of instruction; let her not go: keep her; for she is thy life. Enter not into the path of the wicked, and go not in the way of evil men.

And 20-23

> My son, attend to my words; incline thine ear unto my sayings. Let them not depart from thine eyes; keep them in the midst of thine heart. For they are life unto those that find them, and health to all their flesh. Keep thy heart with all diligence; for out of it are the issues of life.

One most interesting point about leaving ethical wills is that it makes no difference whether the writer is wealthy or of quite modest means, whether male or female, whether highly educated or not. The love and concern for the next generations come through.

It is sad that through the centuries, the ethical will became less popular. It was primarily a Jewish tradition and was for a long time kept active mainly by a few ethnic groups. Now, however, its time is coming again.

NOTES FOR MY ETHICAL WILLS:

NOTES

NOTES

The Baby Boomers Adopt It

The baby boomers, that historically and socially significant group of some 80 million Americans, seem to have latched on to this concept as a way to bequeath their nonmaterial wealth to their children and grandchildren. (Tobin in Baines 2002) They can put on paper for future reference their family history, their personal achievements and struggles, and the ethics and moral guides that led them to the situations in which they now find themselves. It has been said that an ethical will is a window into the soul of the writer. (Flashman, et al) These boomers are happy to leave their valuables to their children, but some can see that those children have not experienced the hard work and careful planning that went into accumulating that fortune.

McAulay addresses a sharp edge of the ethical wills business that has grown up to serve ethical will writers who need some help writing them. It can be an unnecessary expense. To some extent I agree with her, and that is why this book was written to help. You can do an ethical will. Just keep reading, and it will make more and more sense, and soon you will be making notes, outlines, and—eventually—your ethical will.

This ethical will was written to show that a person can accept the concepts of death and dying without being overly emotional or sorrowful. It can provide the sense of closure with friends and relatives who need to let go and say goodbye. We can say goodbye in our own way if we let ourselves be open to experiencing the meaning of the letter that is the writer's ethical will.

As you get your thoughts and feelings on paper, keep in mind, "if the message you leave is from the heart, spelling and grammatical mistakes will be inconsequential to the loved ones reading your words." (Flashman, et all)

Example

Grandma Says Goodbye

For some of you, this is your ma, and for some, your grandma, writing this last letter to all of you in the family. John says it is my ethical will. I don't know about that, but I want to say a few things to you before I meet my maker.

I guess it's vanity, but I need to let you know who I really am. I am older than dirt, so that lets me say what I think. If I get to ranting and raving about some subject dear to your heart, just remember I never mean any personal insult to anyone with a different opinion then mine.

Okay, who am I? I am a child of God, no better then anyone else, but as an American woman, no less than anybody on this earth, neither. I had a friend from kind of a white-trashy background who was taught to say she was "good as anybody, and better 'n most."

I was a good little Midwestern schoolgirl. I got my first seven years of schooling in a two-room school. That was just like the old-fashioned one-room country school, except it was in a very small town and there was a teacher for K-third grades on the lower floor and a teacher for fourth through sixth grades on the second floor. I mention it because I think it had something to do with my behaving how I have for the rest of my life.

That brings up a big point I want to make. If I could form your attitudes toward life, I might start with how you treat others—people and animals and the earth itself. In that school, classes were sometimes small as three students. When I begun school, there was only three of us in Kindergarten, only it wasn't called that. It was "Primary" grade. The three of us were Martha, Jerry, and me. We did the usual stuff—learning to read our numbers and then write them, and coloring lots of shapes the right colors. The crayons were the size of hot dogs and they was way too big to color good enough to stay in the lines. I wasn't ever happy with my pictures. Jerry couldn't stay in the lines at all. He had this little quirk in doing his alphabet. He simply had never heard the names of a few of the letters in the middle. One day we were getting drilled on the letters and I could see he was guessing. When the teacher pointed to the N, he guessed "meadow." I knew right away what he meant. You know how the song goes, "...L M meadow P..." The teacher got mad at him, and I felt sorry for the little guy. I never forgot how bad it can be to not know or understand something in class. That might have been the first time I recognized my ability to be compassionate. A little compassion goes a long way toward understanding folks.

There are so many thoughts I want to give to you, but I probably won't live that long.

That idea is the next thing I had better talk about. The

doctors mostly agree that I won't be here to see Christmas this year. I want you all to listen to this. *It is all right* that I am going on. I cannot be sure what is next, but I am positive there is another experience of some kind awaiting each of us. I am eager to discover mine. Not so eager that I would rush into death by my own hand. And I am not *eager* to leave all of you and the life I have put together for myself and all of you who share a part of it.

When I decided to try to write down my thoughts and warnings, John said I would learn more about myself because I would have to think about what I believed. Then I'd have to write them down. He was dead right. (Joke! That's a little joke.)

I spent a couple of days on how I feel about suicide. For a long time I have supported some reasons for suicide. I believe that for someone so completely out of hope that death seemed the only way out, God has a special way of considering that person's motives and actions. If the person has agonized over the decision and prayed for guidance, then I suppose the answer might come to them that suicide would be right for them.

I briefly thought about it when I began having some very bad days. But In a day or two things always looked better, so I quit thinking about it. I believe that if we listen for the still small voice and follow the ideas that come to us, we are able to handle anything that comes along. God is granting me so much good in my life that it would be selfish and ungrateful to end it.

What good things? Well, blue skies and changing seasons, and kittens, ...charity in our hearts, little green onions and English peas in spring, and tomatoes in August, ...and the view from our west deck, including the horses, the wild turkeys, and the deer, ...and the joy of good neighbors, the satisfaction of hard work, and the comfort of family. That is just a start. Do you have about a year to listen??

Yes, Children of all generations, you are at the top of my

list. Nothing is more important than your happiness, your satisfaction with yourselves, and your secure futures. I love each of you as much as I am capable of loving, and for always. The phrase today is "unconditional." There is nothing you could do that would destroy our love of each other. I can get very angry with some of you sometimes, but I always love you even though I am very disappointed when you don't do as well as you could and should.

But I am far more proud of you all than I am disappointed. Always remember that you come from fine families on both sides. You must not disgrace the family. We can't control the things that can challenge us, but you can avoid many of the bad ones just by sticking with your upbringing.

Your upbringing has included a serious respect for the Ten Commandments. The one that seems to get folks into trouble the quickest these days is the one about telling the truth. It seems to me that if a fella or gal can manage to tell the truth about everything, even to themselves, they would be a whole lot better off than trying to remember the lie they might of told.

I believe that girls should be ladies and boys should be gentlemen. Good manners develop when you try to consider the other fellow first. Lawfulness develops when you obey the spirit of the law as well as the letter of the law. If you disagree, find a legal way to change it. One way is to support candidates who agree with you, or else run for office yourself. Good voting develops when you try to forecast what would allow the greatest good for the greatest number.

Say, I believe I am enjoying this job. No one can argue with me right now. If we read this together while I am still alive, then you may question me, as long as you don't get sassy. I won't have a sassy, mouthy kid around. My own children learned that early, and they have done a good job training the grandchildren. Thank you. They are a joy to have around, and so good to help their grandma when help is needed.

I guess I love those grandchildren about as much as it is possible to love. The old joke is right, though. It is lovely to have them visit, but it is also nice when they go home! Some of them are old enough to remember me, but they won't be too clear as to who I was or what I was like. Will someone please keep a copy of this letter to let them read when they get old enough to be curious? I have put a lot of thought into this so they will know that I wanted to get to know them, but I couldn't wait that long. We'll be together someday.

A word about your dad and granddad. My husband was the finest man I ever knew. He could make me happier than anyone else on earth could. And more frustrated. And more impatient. And more proud and grateful for our family. Did you children all know that I chose all your names after the first child? He liked only one name and he refused to consider any names for the subsequent children we had. So I named you with names that I liked and that honored family members and friends of mine.

He worked hard enough to be successful, but he never really loved his job. He was happiest just going out alone for a drive in the country. He enjoyed playing the piano, and everyone who heard him was impressed and wanted to hear more. Remember that he never looked at a sheet of music? It was all by ear and his talented fingertips.

He memorized so much and worked out his interpretations when he was a teenager, because he practiced his piano when he had to stay indoors. Allergy season for him ran from April until November.

We didn't see eye to eye about some things, but like I said, he was a good man.

I am a little tired from all this lecturing. Maybe I can add some more of my thinking later on. For now, this is enough. And if I never get back to it, you must remember that the old gal had her heart in the right place. And remember that she loved you.

Your Mom and Grandmother

Chapter Two

For Whom is My Ethical Will Created?

The baby boomers also are watching their parents' generation disappearing rapidly. Many are footing the bills for professional writing assistance so their parents can save time and leave their stories and ethical beliefs before it is too late. Lisa Cornwell (2005) observes, "While anyone can jot down their thoughts for family and friends, the formalized ethical wills offer a document more likely to be preserved through the years." There is a discussion of printing options in a later chapter.

Example

General Letters and Individualized Messages

This family is entirely fictional. The dying father writes a general letter to his five children and then adds a personal note to each child.

Dear Tom, Tim, Tyler, Tammy, and Twyla,

I may never before have written all your names on a letter. In fact, I am not sure I ever wrote you a real letter. I guess your mother did the writing when you were off to camp, or college, or boot camp. Once in a while she had me add a line or two as a post script, but she complained that by the time I got around to it, the letter was old news. She was right, of course.

But you kids were all always on my mind. You and your mom have been my life since the day I met her. That was my happiest day, and the four days on which you guys entered the world were the next best.

This letter is just one last way of expressing my love for all of you and your families. I love you all. There, I said it. I probably never said the words often enough, but I think you know how I feel.

We are a family and we make a good team. I hope that after I am gone, you will each make a serious effort to keep in close touch with each other and get together for fun as often as is practical. Be sure to offer support and help with everything that you can. Remember, too, that we all frequently disagree with each other on some matters, but we keep our respect for each other strong and verbal.

The Boy Scout Law makes a pretty good guide for living. If you can say you live up to that group of qualities, you will be fine people, folks that your brothers and sisters are proud to be related to.

After you each have read your copy of this general letter, you will find an individual note in your envelope. You didn't think you'd get off with just this bit of advice did you?

Remember that I am not afraid to go on and see what comes next. I just regret leaving such a beautiful world and my wonderful family and friends. And there is something good to be said about knowing when it is almost time. The doctors say maybe three to four months. Knowing that estimate gave me the time and courage to write these letters to you. Don't be sad for long. Remember the many, many good times and be grateful. Then get together and make some more memories for the grandchildren. And take care of yourselves so you will be around to meet your own great-grandchildren. Goodbye.

Love, Dad

Dear Tom,

This is just a personal note to thank you and admire you for all you do for the family, especially me since my illness set in and made me worthless. You have always been a fine son. It seemed like from the time you were able to understand that you were our firstborn, you have accepted the responsibilities of leadership of your siblings. And that wasn't too easy considering your ten-minute-younger brother!

When you two were six years old, I thought you would never be at peace with each other. Then your mother had to be in the hospital for a week after Tammy was born and we were all so busy with Tyler. Do you recall that he was three years old and frantic because he thought his mom was gone for good? You "older" guys kind of had to fend for yourselves. And within that week you settled your differences somehow and the family has been pretty peaceful ever since.

I admire the man you have become. Carry on. Your own little family is demonstrating the values that you and your lovely Christine live by. Your children are friendly and of a generous spirit. I am proud of my son and daughter-in-law.

The only thing I would ask of you now is that you do whatever you can for your mother. She will get through this mourning period because she is strong in emotion and faith. We understand each other, and the actual parting isn't so bad, but later she will be lonely and the house will seem so quiet after nearly forty years of family activity. I know I don't even have to ask. I just wanted you to know that I know you will be there.

Tom, I am going to close with something you asked me on your thirteenth birthday not to do anymore and I have abided by that request. The reason you were called "Tommy" as a child was because of our names, (Thomas and Yvonne.) We named you all with names containing a T and a Y: Tommy, TImmy, Tyler, Tammy, and Twyla. Sorry, but I cannot resist... Goodbye, Tommy. I love you.

Dad

Dear Tim,

I wanted to write a special personal note to each of you. You are such a loving young man and so good-hearted that you deserve special recognition. I first recognized that you would be calm and satisfied with life the minute after you were born. A certain twin brother of yours was howling in indignation at having been forced out of his warm environment. He squalled for a good twenty minutes. You, on the other hand, were happy to murmur a soft little greeting to your mother and me and then took a nap.

That laid-back attitude has taken you far. I think you are probably the fine teacher you are in part because of your patience and calm expectation of good in your students.

You have always been reliable and kind to the younger kids. We appreciated that. And don't think we didn't know that there were times when you rescued your bossy older brother! Somehow when you were the one explaining, there was no belligerence or sidestepping of the issues. You usually confessed and took your punishment like a man.

And today you stand as a fine man, respected in the community as well as by your family. You don't pay attention, of course. Too modest. And too excited about your first little one coming in just about two months! I have to admit, Timmy, that if I could be granted one last wish, it would be to see the whole family welcome him or her. Let's hope that I will be here for that happy day.

I know that you will see to your mother's comfort and well-being. She is strong and content, but will be a little lonely later on. One of the very best cures for that condition is time with the newest member of the family. You and Jill are going to be wonderful parents, and I know you will share that baby with Grandma.

I feel I am leaving our lovely family in good hands with you older boys still leading and looking out for them. Thanks again. Goodbye, son. I love you.

Dad

Dear Tyler,

These individual notes are so easy to write because you five are so different in personality and interests. You occupy the position of middle child. You are the only boy born as a single birth. It was refreshing to have just one to concentrate on after the somewhat hectic babyhood of the twins. And you were such a welcome and adorable little boy, easy to rear and still giving us great happiness. We had initially wanted three boys and three girls, so you completed the first part of the plan.

You have accomplished most of what you planned to do in life, so far, and we were very pleased with your good judgment and hard work. Becoming an Eagle Scout was important to you and we were so pleased when you attained that rank. A college degree with a high grade point average was your (and our) reward. Your working part time and attending school part time was a bonus since it led to your excellent new job. Forgive me, I should say new position. Ya' done good, kid.

Your marriage seemed to hold such promise and we were devastated when you two chose to end it. But please believe that there is the right woman waiting for you just as you are hoping to meet her. Be patient and have faith.

Since you are in the middle, you probably have the closest relationship to each of your siblings. Please try to use that position to organize plenty of get-togethers among your families. You are already a beloved uncle, so build on that. You mother so thoroughly enjoys all you kids and grandkids when we can all be a together for a holiday or birthday celebration.

I know you will take some time for your mom, alone, as well. Remember she loves going to eat in town after church. It doesn't have to be fancy or take all afternoon. She just wants to spend face-to-face time with her children.

Ty, you are quite the young man. Congratulations. I have no doubt that you will succeed on all levels for the rest of your life. I wish that I could stay a few years longer to share your happiness, but I am grateful for all the times and love we have had through the years.

Goodbye, my son.

Love, Dad

Dear Tammy,

These personalized notes seemed so simple and easy and a pleasure to write... until I began this one-- to my elder daughter.

The difficulty isn't what you probably think. You always have had a tendency to jump to conclusions. Don't jump this time.

First the easy part. You were the finest surprise we had ever seen the morning you were born. For some reason, your mother had an extremely strong notion that you would be little boy number four. And since her intuition had been accurate three times before, I tended to believe it, too. But even then, you had your own way of doing things. You alerted us on a Sunday afternoon that you were coming early. We farmed out the boys and headed to the hospital. By Monday evening, your little joke was evident so we collected the kids and went home. Tuesday evening you tried again; same story. Back at home, all was quiet for another week.

Then, on that Monday, closer to the due date, you began a serious attempt to arrive but just when the labor was getting serious, you backed off again. In a couple more days, you engaged your mother in a battle of wills. She was sure you should quit fooling around and be born, and you seemed to want some extra time. Your mother and the doctor won, but at a cost to your mom. She spent a few days in the hospital with you. I learned it is possible to feed breakfast to two six-year-olds and a whiny three-year-old and still get out to the fields to work by seven in the morning. (Your Aunt Dorene came to watch the boys during the day.)

But you made up for the trouble by being the loveliest baby girl we could want. "Little Tammy Surprise," your mom called you for the first month. All three of your brothers were enchanted. You were carried around so much that we began to wonder if you would ever learn to walk.

You never stopped being a wonderful surprise. We are very proud of you and all you have accomplished. Your art work is spectacular, (Where did you get your talent? We don't think you inherited it!) and you will be an effective art teacher after you graduate next year. Your feeling for people will help you understand their need to express their own feelings. Art is a great way to do that.

Now I think I am ready to put on paper what I feel in my heart. You were expecting me to address your lifestyle negatively, weren't you? I wish I had had more time to let you come to us to tell us. I wish I had more time to sort out my reactions and become comfortable with the idea of losing you to that world that endures so much prejudice and hatred. I wish I had more time with you to let you see that I love you and will always love you no matter who you identify with or select to spend your life with. If it should be Deborah, your current housemate, then she would earn our love and respect simply because she is important to you. If it is someone you will meet in the future, I know she will be a fine person because I know my daughter, and my daughter doesn't accept any junk. I would hope that you commit to a long-term relationship with whomever you choose.

Tammy, your mother may have a little trouble with this concept. Because of the stress that will be created by my death and funeral and the resulting economic adjustments, I hope you will hold off on making it public knowledge in the near future, if you choose ever to make that statement. We have talked about the possibility and I know she will adjust and support you. Her grief over it is not your attitude about marriage and life partners, but over the idea that she will not experience grandchildren from you. I told her that there are alternatives for you, such as adoption. We never know what to expect from our little surprise. You just go on thoughtfully doing whatever you are going to do. We have neither the desire to nor the illusion of stopping or changing you. Just be happy. And if you are going to live so far away in that big city, at least call your mother once a week! I love you, my beautiful daughter. Goodbye.

Dad

Dear Mar,

I know you have a name, but you don't care for it (I like your nickname better, too). Mar rhymes with star and many consider you the shining star of this tribe. Since you are our second daughter and last child, you have always been in the spotlight of your older siblings' attention. They all consider you their baby. Tammy welcomed you as a playmate when all three brothers began to leave her crying in the yard. At least they closed and locked the gate when they ran off! Thank goodness you girls have been close all these growing-up years.

Because of all the attention, little Twyla Marie, you have become the star. You never had a chance to be the boss, like Tom. You haven't developed the patience of Tim since everyone catered to your every whim. You are like Ty in your pursuit of achievements, but you work toward a more personal satisfaction. The roles you played so convincingly on the high school stage should have alerted us to the possibility of a talented actress and an eventual playwright. Your first year of college has commanded the attention of the critics and brought you validation for standing up to us and insisting you be allowed to try a theatre major. You go, girl. You do have the stuff it takes.

But do you have the stuff you need to keep this family in one piece? Will you make every effort to keep in touch regularly? You mother is going to need all her children around her when I die and leave her alone. I know she will be lonely sometimes, but don't like thinking that she will be alone. I have asked the other four to care for her but I think you need a special request and a reminder that you have a responsibility to let her know about your life away from her. She quite naturally considers you the baby of the family, still needing her. You may hate that, but it doesn't make her anguish any less when you fail to keep in touch.

I know that you will do your best. Bring your young man home for a holiday or just a weekend when you are seeing one that you care that much for. I wish I could be there to meet them. Let your mom read the drafts of your plays and other writings. She can keep them confidential and it would mean so much to her. Thanks, Mar.

Have a good life and go on shining, whether as an actress or an author or maybe someday when you leave your work for a few years to be a wife and stay-at-home mother. When you go back to the stage you will have added that quality called experience and will be a better performer because of it.

I am pleased to be the father of the star, Mar. Goodbye, and break a leg.

I love you, Dad

The list of recipients may shrink or grow as you immerse yourself in your project. You probably will find yourself adjusting the content as well as the form and tone. One outcome that many writers of their ethical wills have in common is the development of a sense of themselves. They discover a depth to their own personalities. They define more sharply the dreams that had always just floated freely in their minds during the moments they allowed themselves to daydream.

It seems that it is the 50-something to 60-something age group who can benefit the most from the activity of writing ethical wills. They have had a variety of experiences in their lifetime. Some of that experience had to have resulted in some learning. We might even say they have acquired a great deal of practical knowledge. And it isn't stretching it to credit these mature adults with that highly-prized quality called wisdom.

They know and remember what they came up from and worked their way through to earn their spot in society. But at an age sometimes less than retirement age, they can foresee a long life ahead of them. They have little reluctance to share their wisdom through advice and stories. They know themselves in relation to their society and they recognize their value to that very society.

In a sense, the ethical will is a present the baby boomers give to themselves and to each other. As they think and remember their past, and the family history, (as much of it as they have been told,) they begin to match up the principles they stand for with that history. Their reflections could foster a deep and perhaps spiritual respect for the continuing power of good in their lives. What a tremendous influence that concept could be upon the boomers' children and grandchildren!

As the boomers write their history and tell their stories and plan the ethical will they want to leave, they often find themselves wanting to act on those very concepts. Many come to a realization that it is not too late to demonstrate to their heirs the ideas they had thought they would relay to them. Instead of leaving them their basic values, they have the opportunity of leading the subsequent two generations in application of those basic values.

Example

Ellie Chauffeurs Her Grandpa

Joe's granddaughter has begun hinting that she really, really wants a new car for her birthday in seven months when she turns seventeen. She knows that her well-to-do grandfather could buy her the whole car dealership if he wanted to, so why not wheedle and plead for a new car?

Grandpa Joe already knows that he will set her up with a cute, clean, safe, well-maintained used car when the birthday rolls around, but he couldn't sleep well if he yielded to her emotional battering.

After some thought, Joe decides on this short letter explaining one of his shortcomings and asking her help to remedy it.

Dear Ellie,

Your not-so-subtle request for a new sports car for your birthday has reached Grandpa's tired old ears. I have taken it under consideration.

In my day, we wouldn't have thought to utter a desire for a new car, let alone ask for one! But I am glad you feel comfortable enough with me to ask. And I am comfortable enough with my retirement income and my shares of stock in our family company to say no if that is what I decide. I worked too hard as a young man to earn it; now that I am a wealthy old man, I decide thoughtfully how to dispose of it.

I have been meaning to ask you something, Ellie. Your mother tells me you have lost interest in most of the school activities offered after school. I can't say that I am unhappy to hear that because I think many of them are make-work projects to keep kids busy so they stay out of trouble. That is just my opinion.

My question is, would you have two hours after school twice a week through this coming semester to spend with me? I need a driver for a volunteer project that I always wanted to do and I still feel that I should do. I feel I might have missed a good thing in life-- volunteering.

I would like to work as a volunteer at two different retirement homes in town, reading books and mail to the residents and helping them with letters and cards that they want to send.

If you volunteered, too, we could reach twice as many folks. It would give you driving practice and I could judge for myself if a car would survive your use and ownership! Please remember my heart condition!

Think it over, Ellie. It would be a four-month commitment that we would stick to as closely as humanly possible.

I am looking forward to getting to

know the emerging adult granddaughter
who had so much fun with me as a little
tomboy when we went fishing years ago.

Love,

Grandpa

Joe could donate money to his pet project and be admired for his generosity. Yet when he was ready to write those sentiments to a self-centered young lady, it dawned on him that it wasn't too late to do it himself. By doing it himself, he demonstrated his sincerity and introduced his granddaughter to the joy of helping others. There was more of Joe in that action than there was of Joe's money. And what will Ellie remember? The first of many vehicles in her lifetime, yes, but also the time she invested in her grandfather's ideas. Later she will be grateful for the time her busy and successful grandparent invested in her.

Joe's ethical will to Ellie was off to a great start. Later, in adding to it, he thanked her for his dependable ride to the retirement homes, her work with the elderly residents, and her commitment to one of his lifelong values--helping others who are not able to do for themselves.

Financial Planners

Some financial planners are beginning to see the value of the ethical will and have begun arranging writing advice and assistance for their clients. Learning something about a client's values, opinions, and philosophy of life helps the financial and estate advisors structure the right plans. They have a better idea of what the client wants to do about things like charitable giving, trust funds, or turning over control.

Legal Influence

Ethical wills carry little or no legal influence over the dispersal of material things, but are intended to convey to the recipients the thoughts, feelings, love, forgiveness, wishes, and advice from the writer. These governing values can be written to children, grandchildren, siblings, other family members, friends, community members, church friends, or anyone specified by the ethical will writer.

Just as the conventional last will and testament allows a parent to assign the family heirlooms to the children, an ethical will is employed to offer advice, thoughts, attitudes, and sentiments to each of the children according to the needs perceived by the parent.

Until the last forty or fifty years, some of the teaching of the ethical standards of a family was done by nearby relatives, especially grandparents. After World War II, many young couples moved some distance from their nuclear families and established the next generation. Sally Hume (Steele) says, "The ethical will strikes a chord with anyone, of any faith. One of the reasons may be the isolation of families, and the mobility of generations. Grandparents aren't around their grandchildren as they were when generations lived closer together. That scattering and lack of familial contact creates a void and fewer opportunities to pass along family tradition and values." A minister named Greg Ward, who teaches classes about ethical wills, explains, "It's a matter of values clarification. Writing an ethical will provides an opportunity for self-assessment and asking what values you want to end up with at the close of our life that you ultimately want to hand off to your loved ones."

Dr. Barry K. Baines, rising star and expert on modern ethical wills says, "...an ethical will written to a child will provide a foundation of common values upon which to approach childrearing. (An) ethical will can help in conflict resolution by increasing the mutual understanding of the parents' values. Even in a divorce situation, it can create security and reassurance of the children involved by providing tangible evidence of what's most important to their parents."

A Unique Gift

You alone are able to leave for those you love this greatest gift you will ever give. This is an opportunity to write a spiritual legacy to your family. Only they are able to receive this greatest gift they will ever accept. It is by nature a very personal and beautiful exchange. It shows a part of you that is not allowed to appear in a formal will or estate plan.

The Reverend Thomas Owen-Toole (2005) feels more can be done to share our values and decisions.

> "Failure to pass on ethical wisdom is a common familial plight. As a professional who does grief counseling, I am troubled by the amount of unfinished business at the time of death, especially between parents and children."

Are the concepts promoted by the ethical will writer accepted by the heirs? Not always.

Rev. Owen-Toole is a realist when he considers some aspects of the handing down of values:

> Tradition literally means that something has been placed in my hands and I, in turn, am urged to pass it on carefully. Of course, once someone has

gifted me with a tradition, I have the right and responsibility to handle it in my own fashion. I can let it be or modify it or drop it or pass it on. Finally, I stand back and permit others to do with it as they choose...as parents, we share things with our children, our most precious gifts, and then you handle them in your own ways.

Others may read the ethical will you have left to an individual, but it will never mean the same thing to them. This is your opportunity to convey those private dreams and memories to the ones whom you choose to tell. This brings up a complication to writing ethical wills: You may find it is difficult to stop.

It is difficult to stop writing after you have begun one to someone. You will have so much to say. But reason and organization must prevail. For an ethical will that takes the form of a letter, a limit of three subjects is advised. More concepts than that can become confusing and indistinguishable.

Example

Grandfather to Grandson

A grandfather realizes he may not be around to see his grandson grow to manhood, so he writes a few lines that Jimmy can keep and look at occasionally through the coming years.

Dear Jimmy,

You are seven years old now and old enough to remember some things about your old grandpa. I will be sorry to leave you when the time comes because I love being with you so much. We have some good times, don't we? Maybe you will remember going with me to pick up the donuts for Saturday morning brunch. Or maybe it will be the summer fishing we did at the pond in the park. I enjoyed your company because you are such a polite little boy and so full of questions. You just keep on asking those questions, Jim. Someday you will experience great satisfaction in finding answers for yourself. I have always enjoyed reading and learning, so I wish that joy for you.

Maybe you will remember my cap collection. After I am gone, you grandchildren may each choose five caps for your own. There will be plenty to choose among, because I am still collecting them and I am not gone yet! (One hint to keep you out of trouble... try to remember not to wear your cap in the house, especially at the table. For some reason, it drives the women in this family a little crazy.)

You are learning something in Sunday School that can be the best set of rules you will ever follow. You know already what it is, don't you? That is right...the Ten Commandments. I am sorry to say that I didn't follow every one of them every day of my life, but I wish I had. If you do your best to follow them, you will be a fine man and you can look back at your life and honestly say you did your best. I will be proud of you just as I am proud of you now. I love you, James.

Your old grandpa,

James Eldred Smith

A letter can be expanded to accommodate more ideas if it is arranged in segments. However, if you get to that point, it may be just as well to call them chapters and give them better organization and chapter headings.

The following excerpt from the ethical will of a serious young man is one of my favorites. I like the concept, I like the content, and I like the ease of understanding it.

Where There's a Will

Bob Perks

When I read my will, there was no "me" there! ...This was a formal listing of all the things of my life. it was indeed a legal document declaring who gets what and how much...

"But where am I in all of this?" I asked myself.

I wasn't there. So, I sat down and created what is called an "Ethical Will." It is not a legal document, but a listing of my own personal beliefs and ideals...

To my children, family and friends,

When you come across a trinket of mine tucked away in a drawer, what will you remember of me? Nothing...

When the final check arrives from the insurance company, ...what will it say to you? Nothing. My will says nothing about who I am. So this is what I want you to know. This is what I want you to remember about me when I'm gone.

Did you know...?

I was sentimental. Old songs, romantic movies, and happy endings made me cry.

I leave for you a sense of caring.

I loved the sunshine bu/
too.

I leave for you a des
everything.

I stopped my car to
I thought there was
seeing one.

I leave you a positive attitude ana ..
search for beauty when it's not obvious.

I often stopped to help someone stranded on
the roadside.

I leave for you compassion.

I paid for the meals of perfect strangers just
because I thought God wanted me to and I did it
anonymously.

I leave for you the sound of the still small voice
within to guide you in things of the heart.

I wanted to be a famous singer more than
anything else...

I leave for you the soul of a dreamer and the
ability to know when to change.

I loved all kinds of music.

I leave for you the ability to take one single note
and hear the symphony within it.

d from jobs at least three times in my
h time it took me in a new direction.

e a sense of adventure and a spirit of
ss.

I loved butter pecan ice cream, chocolate cake
with vanilla icing, turkey dinners with all the
trimmings, and chocolate-covered cherries.

I leave you the vision of life as a feast and God
at the head of the table.

Each time the phone rang I'd smile when I
heard your voice.

Be someone's reason to smile.

I would have done anything for you if you had
asked me.

Be ready to give all you have to all who need.

I had friends all over the world.

I leave for you the desire to make friends of
strangers and a world without borders.

It is a will that measures the things of one's life,
but love that measures the man.

I love you all.

NOTES

NOTES

Chapter Three

Why Am I Leaving
My Ethical Will?

The following piece is condensed from an internet article.

Ethical Wills: A Memory That Keeps on Giving

Kevin H. Crenshaw

...Imagine what it would mean to you to have some words of encouragement or wisdom from a loved one (who) is no longer with you.

In the precarious world we live in, many people have asked that question and decided to take decisive action in the new option called an "ethical will."

This is not a legal document in and of itself; rather it is a public record of our nonrepresentational wealth. It is a way to concretely pass on those things that may be otherwise inaccessible or even forgotten. In much the same way that parents would like to see that their children are financially provided for in their absence, some are leaving emotional and philosophical provisions, as well.

...Ethical wills range in size from a few paragraphs to volumes long and can be in multimedia formats...

...I was introduced to this latest trend at an estate planning conference.... There are three main purposes for ethical wills:

1) leaving an intangible legacy,

2) personal satisfaction, and

3) their utility during the estate planning process.

First, bequeathing ideals...is not a new concept...you may want to consider the value of your life lessons, beliefs, and experiences.

Second, the process of creating an ethical will is personally beneficial, and can be comforting and encouraging to your loved ones. (It is) cathartic to truly reflect on life and what you had learned or nearly forgotten....it focuses on the positive aspects of your experiences.

Finally, there is a legal utility for ethical wills. Increasingly, attorneys are suggesting that their clients have one made in conjunction with their Last Will and Testament and other end-of-life documents. An ethical will can assist an attorney in executing the affairs of your estate in a manner that is agreeable with your values and interests. It can also be used to support or offer a basis for intent in a variety of probate matters such as legal funding and asset distributions. When an attorney has access to your ethical will, they can better personalize your legal matters.

Ethical wills go beyond concepts of either law or morality. They are not just for the religious, nor are they simply for those with extensive estate planning. Consider it as a memory that will live forever. (Crenshaw)

Also found on the internet was a summary of the concept that "an ethical will can be a vehicle for maintaining or even repairing family ties." Charles W.

Collie (Elbaum 2004), working as the ser
advisor at Harvard University, is familia
and effects of wealth in multi-generation

He focuses on the family's wealth
finances, but in family wealth-- as he ider......es it. That
wealth consists of the family's individual members
(human capital), the manner in which the family
communicates, learns, and decides things (intellectual
capital), and the family's relationship to society at large
(social capital).

After 25 years of assisting families in their planning
for the future, he concluded that "families that enhance
human, intellectual, and social capital are more likely
than others to produce great human beings, and
continue as a cohesive group that enjoys meeting and
being together for more than one generation."

Collier thinks the key is in the communication. The
telling of the family's important stories and the
mentoring relationship between generations are two
concepts promoted by the ethical will. McMillen makes
this observation, "It's not only *who gets the
grandfather's clock*, but *who was grandfather?*"

Tax attorney and estate planner Ken Wheeler
writes,

The appeal of an ethical will may be stronger in affluent families, particularly if money has played a divisive role in intrafamily relationships. Most financial advisers are familiar with individuals who earned their fortunes at the expense of relationships with family members. Often monetary rewards lose their importance as people age, and ethical wills offer an opportunity to address past feelings. The older they get, the more they realize that the pursuit of money and having money is not as important as other things.

The Donor Legacy Statement

The term "ethical will" is so nebulous that a few new names are being introduced and employed to try to differentiate among them. A newsletter called *Family Giving News* presents *this financial-oriented list of items* that an ethical will might include, but they prefer to call it the *donor legacy statement*:

a list of advisors, attorneys, accountants, and other financial managers

a list of assets: investments, properties, life insurance policies, bank accounts

a list of debts

general information: social security number, date and place of birth

a family history

a general personal history

a personal statement detailing the person's

greatest wisdoms, biggest regrets, and/or moments of triumph

Let's elaborate on the concept of using an ethical will to define the will-maker's own attitudes toward wealth. From the same newsletter:

> Although similar in spirit to ethical wills, donor legacy statements record history, values, hopes, and dreams of family foundation founders and their boards. These statements are typically intended to guide and inform the ongoing grants and activities of the foundation, and serve as a compass in times of uncertainty.

Since it serves as a tool to help conceptualize the next steps toward the long-term intentions for a family foundation or scholarship or other philanthropic endeavor, the donor legacy helps to determine that the original impetus is maintained. The sentiments and values that led to the establishment of the foundation can prepare the next governing board with good reminders of whatever reason the founders created the instrument. Periodic review of the legacy statement allows the memories and values to remain meaningful and useful in decision-making.

One more list is given to suggest things that could be included in a donor legacy statement. They seem to be more personal.

the donor's life and accomplishments

the causes the donor is interested in (generally or with reference to specific organizations) that grow out of that background

the values, traditions, and perspectives that animate the donor's life and giving history

the resulting specific intent of the donor for the foundation

the way the donor wishes succeeding generations of trustees to perpetuate his legacy over time.

When would be best time to write the donor legacy statement? Probably during the actual development of the financial instrument of philanthropy. It would then represent the original goals. It could always be altered or added to later if the concepts are seen to have changed.

Another use for the ethical will is to inform a prospective life partner of the ethics and morals and expectations of an individual. While optimum age for ethical wills is probably from about 45 to 100, young adults contemplating married life together could benefit from writing a combined ethical will to their approaching marriage. Baines suggests, "People getting married could take a look at it, and clergy could ask the engaged couple to write an ethical will (to) help the couple clearly understand each other's values, and it can contribute to building a foundation of common values for the marriage."

Expanding on the Legal Will

An increasing number of estate lawyers and financial planners are recommending that clients write their feelings and intentions to provide the reasoning that cannot be conveyed by a legal last will and testament. The ethical will can help maintain family harmony.

As a young family was settling a parent's estate, they found that they needed a more personal concept to help demonstrate what the material possessions symbolized. They also wanted to convey to their children how much the concept of a lasting marriage meant to them. They hoped to show their support for any life partnership the children chose in the future if the partnership is based on deep love and commitment. So they included the story of how the wife's mother paused before giving her blessing to their engagement to ask the husband-to-be to promise he would never intentionally hurt her in any way. They could see that if they weren't there to extract such a promise from their children's intended spouses, perhaps the children would value themselves highly enough that they wouldn't settle for just anyone who didn't respect them and care for them emotionally, spiritually, and physically. That one family story had contributed several values to be handed down. (Teicher, 2004)

Experts agree that the documents (wills) should remain separate. An ethical will, unlike a material will, is not a binding, enforceable document. Its contents cannot be objectively quoted, but can help explain-- either directly or indirectly--the thought processes behind the terms of the material will.

If Great Aunt Jane had a reason that she left one twin a valuable piece of furniture and the other twin only a box of books, it would soothe some hurt feelings if her ethical will explained Aunt Jane's thinking. It might be that Jane thought that Nan liked house decorating more than reading. Or she needed to alert Jan that five of her books were rare first editions that would need proper atmospheric storage conditions. Even little things take on a great deal of importance if they are the last communications from a relative.

And remember, not all the sentiments left for the heirs are warm and wonderful.

Two copies of this note were handwritten in Jane's beautiful penmanship.

Example

Auntie Jane's Legacy

Dear Nan and Jan,

I suppose you two are tired of sharing everything. I am writing this note to you together, but at least you will each get a copy. I just want this last communication with you after I have gone on.

As I write, I remember the interesting times we had the summer you were seven years old and stayed a week with me. It was a joy for me; perhaps a little boring for you. Well, perhaps--very boring. You both were very well-behaved. I was glad to discover the municipal swimming pool. If we had not, you two would have spent the whole week whining because I did not have a television!

I am letting you know that I have made my decision about what to leave you in my will. You have been wonderful little nieces through the years. Since I had no children of my own, I used to fantasize that you were both named after me. I don't think that was the case, but it pleased me to think so. My actual first name is Nancy...Nancy Jane.

I would like for Nan to have the French armoire because it provides a place to hang up her coat as soon as she gets into the house. It is never too late to correct a bad habit.

Jan shall inherit my most valuable books because she probably will benefit from reading a few classics and may even enjoy them. I am enclosing directions for the proper care of the wardrobe as well as the proper storage of the fragile books.

If I leave you with a small improvement in character, I have succeeded. Thank you for your respect and love all these years.

Auntie Jane

To repeat, ethical wills are not always pleasant reminders of childhood. They can serve a serious purpose.

Ethical wills are a way to share our values, blessings, life's lessons, hopes and dreams for the future, love, and forgiveness with our family, friends, and community.

Personal Benefits of Writing My Ethical Will

Barry K. Baines' book (p.20-21) includes the thoughtful lists of reasons below:

Creating an ethical will is a way to

- learn about myself

- reflect on my life
- affirm myself
- affirm what others mean to me
- articulate what I stand for
- tell stories that illustrate my values
- tell stories for perpetuity

An ethical will is a forum in which to:

- fill in knowledge gaps of will recipients by providing historic or ancestral information that links generations, conveys feelings, thoughts, and "truths" that are hard to say face-to-face
- express regrets and apologies
- open the door to forgiving and being forgiven
- come to terms with my mortality

Writing an ethical will may be:

- a spiritual experience that provides a sense of completion to my life
- a loving undertaking that helps my loved ones "let go" when my time comes

Diane Currier, a trusts and estates lawyer, finds that a common situation arises where a will distributes differing portions to the heirs. An explanation in an ethical will can ease feelings of resentment and misunderstanding about the division of valuables. She goes on to explain, "A legal will provides the who, what, when, and how of an estate plan, and an ethical will can provide the "why."

In addition to these valuable benefits, there is an immediate benefit as one finishes the ethical will: it makes the writer feel really good. The why factor can help preserve family harmony.

One writer felt both uplifted and empowered by the exercise and discipline of constructing her ethical will and the self-reflection was a key to realizing that she had a legacy of strength and a survival instinct and many personal assets. (Elbaum)

NOTES

Ethical Wills Gain Favor

Michael Paulson

Like any responsible parent with a lot of money, yogurt king Gary Hirshberg is writing a will. But the... CEO is going further, writing a second document explaining to his children why he does things (as he does.)

Hirshberg is at the leading edge of a new estate planning trend. He is writing a so-called ethical will, or legacy statement, to make sure he leaves behind not just valuables, but values.

"I would like a written record and road map of what my wife and I were trying to do, so when there's a big check for the kids, they know where it came from, and why," he said. "I want them to understand where this came from, and to inspire them to think..."

Increasingly, as baby boomers seek to bequeath more than material goods to the next generation, they are scripting documents that spell out their own stories--how they became who they are, what was important to them, what they want for the future.

The wills tend to be part family history, part personal story, and part an explication of a person's value system. Some include advice or suggestion, but specialists generally frown on any attempt to reach beyond the grave and instruct heirs as to how to behave...

There has been a resurgent interest in ethical wills, spurred by the aging of baby boomers, the rising interest in family history, and the increased affluence in society that forces many people to realize they will be leaving their heirs a lot of money.

Estate lawyers and financial planners are increasingly suggesting ethical wills as part of estate planning for clients...

(One client) said, "Being in your business and being successful and passing all the wealth down is one thing. But all you've earned, all your philosophies, all your experiences, how do they get passed down?"...(My ethical will) is about us, our family, how we started, why we started, what drove us, and what we think is important in running a business. There is no formula for success, but one element of success is do the right thing morally and ethically and that will carry you," he said.

"People are realizing there's more to life than material things, and they want to tap into things that are transcendent in nature," said Dr. Barry K. Baines, (2002) the Minneapolis physician who became an advocate of ethical wills as a way of helping hospice residents prepare for death.

NOTES

Chapter Four

What Precautions Should I Take?

Please realize the power of your ethical will. It will be cherished and valued by all the recipients who are able to comprehend the love and the labor that went into it just so you could leave to them your thoughts about them. If they are grieving your death when they receive your ethical will, it may very likely ease the emptiness they feel as a result of your passing. It may make the probation of your last will and testament easier. It may grant you a peaceful feeling about the situation you are leaving behind.

Emotional Issues

We should also consider the problems that an ethical will could possibly create. The one about which I am a little bit concerned involves you, the creator of the ethical will.

There is a very slight possibility that you could uncover some traumatic incident in your life that you had blocked or simply forgotten. Actively making an effort to remember things, pleasant and/or important, which you want to recall in detail for your loved one could possibly bring up memories that you had put away.

If you are aware of this improbable turn of events, you will be forewarned. What should you do if something you remember makes you uncomfortable? You have choices. You can call on the experts for help. A family therapist will be most willing to sit down with you and try to discover with you the subject and the resulting discomfort. Then s/he can guide you to working it out.

You may decide to face it and let someone know about it. You may decide it was important at the time, but that you are years more mature and can deal with it now by accepting that it happened. You may allow yourself some righteous anger or pain or sorrow. You may be able to correct the mistake or confront the individual who did you wrong or, if it was your error, apologize to your victim. A professional counselor asks the right questions and you can work out of the discomfort of remembering.

Another source of help is your minister or rabbi or other spiritual guide. Tell him/her what you are doing and what has happened. Again, the problem can be faced in an appropriate way and dealt with. If the source of your problem is an individual who is able to discuss it with you and you feel independent enough to deal with him/her, then perhaps it is time to have it out. This should be carefully considered. You don't want to go off unprepared.

You can always attempt to stuff the problem thoughts back in the box they escaped from, but it won't be as comforting as facing them and dealing with them. Finding out why you become uncomfortable as a result of remembering is important to your emotional well-being. The troubling memories can't be set aside easily, and probably shouldn't be. If you find yourself being traumatized by the memories you have uncovered, call for help. It isn't likely. Most people experience mostly pleasure in their memories. It is good to go back to the years gone by. There are some events that you will regret or feel sorry about, but that was part of your life and had some part in making you the person you are today.

On the positive side, the writer of an ethical will is able to consider his life experiences, point out the meaning of them as best he can, define his morals and ethics, and give his heirs his blessings. On the negative side, there are writers who use the ethical will as a tool to control his or her heirs, especially after his or her death. To create an ethical will that honors his own life as well as those of his family, the writer must avoid creating or stirring up guilt or trying to control things from the grave. "There's a temptation to try to criticize, cause guilt, or tell people how to behave..." (Reimer)

The Robb report gives this advice for creating an ethical will that will be appreciated and treasured long after you are gone: Do not be rash. Plan it, taking your time to avoid working on it if you are unhappy with a family member. Reread it annually to make necessary changes. Let yourself feel when the time is right to present it. Even after presentation, it can be a work in progress until you die, if you'd like to go on that long. Keep it separate from your last will and testament. Don't try to advise or require money transactions, but it is okay to ask that your values be considered.

There are plenty of positive ideas to include in your ethical will.

There is almost no limit to the amount or type of information that can be included in an ethical will. Contents might include insights into happiness, business success, dealing with difficult times and difficult people. Historical information that might otherwise be forever lost can be transmitted. For example, the circumstance surrounding meeting a spouse, delivery of a child, overcoming adversity, or the memories from a particular trip or moment of time. Recounting major lifetime decisions, and the purposes underlying those decisions, might also be included. Recommendations about favorite books, songs, or movies might be important for some to share for posterity. (Friedman)

Whether you are a parent or a small business owner, the most valuable assets you can leave your children, your clients, and the community are your own insights, knowledge, and wisdom.

Legal Issues

If you are planning a blockbuster revelation, please reconsider. On a personal note, do you want to be remembered for your troubling revelations that may harm living people after you have slipped these earthly bonds? Perhaps there was a good reason that some "facts" were never revealed. Some truths should be told, but only *certain individuals* have the right to dispense the information to people *they* choose, at the time *they* feel is right, *if at all*. Nobody made you the omniscient secret-revealer. Think about your place, your power, and the people involved.

If you are still considering "setting some things straight," I strongly urge you to consult a lawyer about what to say and how to say it to avoid the probable lawsuits resulting from libel. It is not possible to go into specifics in an introductory book like this, but there is room for this strong warning: *Do not use a beautiful concept like the ethical will to further your own private agenda, win your old arguments, or indulge in malicious, hurtful gossip. If you do, it may backfire at you and you could find yourself unable to prove in court the very facts you meant to reveal.* Hello, huge financial litigation settlements and maybe jail time!

Standards and Practices

After all this encouragement to get going on your memories and advice, we will slow down briefly to consider the rules or standards that critics are beginning to voice.

A controversy is growing over the definition of memoirs. When the reader picks up a memoir to read, s/he deserves to know how truthful it is. But whose truth? Clark says that memoirs have at least two main groups. Those that stick to traditional standard of factuality should probably be called non-fiction memoirs. But a narrative form of memoir depends on the imagination (for dialog) and interpretation (for activities.) Many contemporary writers blatantly fabricate fiction and pseudo-memories and call it a memoir, with no real concern for authenticity. The best we can credit them with is "based on a true story."

This is labeling memoirs according to the strategies employed to write them. A third category has developed in modern journalism. It is referred to as the "transparency" style. The author uses disclaimers and a declaration of the methods used in compiling facts and the standards by which it was written.

There is a fourth critical part to memoir writing *and publishing*, but it applies less to the private ethical will than to the family writers. Writings destined for publication should be fact-checked by an independent fact editor. Readers deserve that consideration. This applies to you, the writer of private thoughts and advice, only to the extent that you respect your recipients, the heirs to your ethical will. Make it as accurate as you possibly can. And be generous with phrases that keep you honest, like, "to the best of my recollection," or "as they told the story..." or "It must have been..."

May I Write Another's Ethical Will?

This last precaution isn't here to keep you out of jail, but in the hearts and respect of other folks who loved the same individual you might like to speak for. Or write for. Sometimes we think we know the loved one so well that we can create the ethical will she or he would have left for us if she or he had done the writing.

Think about that. No one should speak for another in serious matters such as how to be remembered. I have borrowed and edited slightly a nice example of a son trying to write an ethical will for his father. I approve the effort because he says he *thinks* it would be what his dad *might* have written. Before he read it at his father's funeral, he asked several people close to him if they felt it was accurate.

Writing Dad's Ethical Will

If Dad had written an ethical will, I think this would be it…

Dear Family and Friends,

I am leaving you with what matters most to me and what I hope you remember most.

1ˢᵗ and foremost is the love of family, They are the wellspring of who you are. Nurture the relationships, be there for each other.

Dad was always there for his mother, brother and sisters, When he married, he added his in-laws as part of his family. When we married, he refused to be considered an in-law, he was Dad and our spouses were his children.

2ⁿᵈ Value education and life long learning. It keeps you stimulated, keeps you young, and helps you succeed.

3ʳᵈ Give to your community. We all come out of a community, were enriched by it, and have the responsibility to give back to the community.

4ᵗʰ, Whatever you do, work hard, play hard and compete hard at both.

And finally, friends and family (he would have written) never lose your sense of humor; remember not to take yourself so damn seriously.....

As I said to Dad this past Friday, when I think about how to handle my kids, I ask— what would Dad do?

He never wrote it down, but through his actions he left us a very clear ethical will. (Baines 1998)

Perhaps we find it acceptable because the son keeps it in very general and positive terms and uses it in praise of his father. For the most part, ethical wills should be written by the individual. The son's own ethical will could include the same sentiments and praise, but would not step over the line of personal work.

This ghostwritten ethical will must have been entirely appropriate, because everyone attending the funeral asked for a copy by which to remember Dad.

NOTES

NOTES

Chapter Five

How Do I Begin My Ethical Will?

If you understand and accept the potential value of your ethical will, you will want to begin it as soon as is practical because we never know how much time there will be for the writer as well as the recipients. You won't want to rush it because there is so much thinking that goes into it, but please make it a priority.

The Five Steps in Writing Your Ethical Will

The following five general steps will help you get organized.

1. Willingness to write your Ethical Will

Think over your reasons and expectations for writing.

2. Preparation to write

How will you approach it?

What format do you favor?

How lengthy is it likely to be?

3. Actions to take

Write a list of things to say to your family, friends, community, church congregation, etc. Will one Ethical Will serve for all those purposes?

Begin by writing your rough draft.

Polish it until the writing says just what you feel and want your heirs to know about you.

4. Completion

Decide on the physical presentation of your Ethical Will.

Will it be written as letters, or will you need a book for all your thoughts, advice, and wishes? A bound book or a three-ring notebook?

Anticipate your duplication or printing and binding needs.

5. Review/Renewal

If you choose to wait for a later presentation, make a schedule for reviewing your Ethical Will periodically. You may want to add to it or change the wording as your family conditions change. Some members marry into the family, some pass from it, and some are born into it. You may want to make some changes.

To elaborate on each of these steps:

1. Willingness

I feel so strongly about the content and use of ethical wills that I was promoting them before I even had heard them called ethical wills! I'd like to quote an idea from my earlier (1999) book, *Passing Your Heritage On: A Guide to Writing Your Family Stories.* The first chapter is called, "What Stories Should I Tell, and Why?" On page six, I had encouraged my readers to adopt an "ethical wills" philosophy.

I believe that one of the finest outcomes of these family stories is the telling and showing of strong family-related values and beliefs. They were so instrumental in shaping us and our lives that they should be explained and honored.

The future generations should know and understand the important ideas you have lived by. Your stories encourage them to reconsider the ideas with an open mind. Hearing how your traditional values served you well throughout your lifetime can only enhance those values in the minds of readers. Your grandchildren will appreciate knowing them as they discover their self-identities and begin coping with some of the same problems you encountered years ago. They may even maintain some of your traditional values.

As you write your stories, you might look for ways to incorporate the values you'd like to promote. Be sure not to oversell. If they come into the tale naturally, they will make a better impression...

What are your reasons for leaving your thoughts to your loved ones? Do you wish to leave an expression of your personality? Do you want to give your point of view about things—politics, religion, business ethics, moral issues, use of money (capital, investments, entertainment, trusts, etc.) or family loyalty? The possibilities are endless. Will your code of ethics change in various situations?

2. Preparation

As you think about beginning your ethical will, you could take the opportunity to collect things that will jog your memory, things that are important to show or explain or give. These could range from favorite photographs to a long-intended apology. Some folks do better just sitting down with pen and paper and starting to write, but I prefer the concept of preparing for such an important task. Psychologist Carol Kauffman advises, "Ethical wills are not for the weak of heart. You have to sit down, think of your life as a finite experience, and try to convey in writing what is most important to you." (Robb Report)

There are those willing writers who would like to try

it, but "what may seem a simple matter can be quite daunting to those who have tried to sum up a lifetime of values and beliefs, some of which may have been shifted or changed dramatically over the years." (Morphew)

Soon you will be making notes so you won't leave anything out. An outline is so easily changed by adding or rewording parts of it, especially on a computer. Loose-leaf pages for a notebook are also easily removed or changed.

This preparation phase is a time to just relax and let the ideas come to you. If they don't come easily, ask yourself some questions and give the answers. Your letter begins to write itself. What gives you pride as you look back? What are you ashamed of? Regrets? If you miss the old days, what do you miss? People? Activities? Chores? Pets?

You will be able to make some early decisions. What form should this very important communication take? The written word is one of the most permanent forms to employ, but there are many others. The most modern would probably be a videotape of yourself speaking to the camera and telling your stories and feelings. That tape could be transferred to a digital form of DVD or whatever is the newest invention at the time. There is a theory that the electronic forms are more fragile and more likely to become obsolete. It would be most frustrating to your future generations if they encounter problems finding the right machine to play the ethical will that their great-great-grandfather recorded for them. If videotaping or the multimedia format appeals to you, there are professional videographers and personal historians who specialize in creating them. The Association of Personal Historians (APH) includes a section of videographers. (See Appendix Three) They would be happy to discuss their work with you.

> Some people choose to keep their ethical wills in video form but consultants often encourage writing because of the thought process it involves, and because video recordings may be harder for future generations to access as technology changes. Whatever the form, an ethical will can be kept with the last will and testament, but some choose to give it its own place—perhaps, even a special box, so they can show it to family members or update it more easily... (Rehl)

I believe that most people could write an ethical will by themselves. But since it is very personal and complicated, many would-be writers feel they can't do it, so they don't try. For that reason, consultants for hire are establishing themselves in business to assist their clients in writing their ethical wills or will write them for their clients. (Again, try the APH.)

You have the opportunity to be very creative, perhaps even writing poetry or songs to convey the ideas you want to leave your family. Your ethical will could be centered on a magnificent scrapbook with various photos and mementos that were each explained or demonstrated in different ways: slide shows, old home movies transferred to videotape, selected background music, explanations in the original storytellers' voices on a recorded tape or digital recordings, original songs and poetry, artwork by the family members, etc.

"There is no single right way to draft an ethical will. Just make sure it comes from the heart," says Baines, "and don't malign your heirs.'"

3. Action

After your preparation, you will want to write a list of things to say to your family, to your friends, to the community, to your church congregation, etc. You may well find that one ethical will isn't appropriate for all those purpose. Now is the time to set your priorities. I would assume your message to the family would come first.

You might begin by referring to my long list of words in Appendix Two, words that are often found in an ethical will. The subject of ethics covers such a wide band of rules and attitudes. You will also find a few common phrases that are popular. They will help you decide what to include and some of the ways you can word the ideas you are using.

Begin by writing your rough draft. Polish it until the writing says just what you are feeling and want to let your heirs know about you.

4. Completion

Decide on the physical presentation of your Ethical Will. Will it be written as a letter or will you need a book for all your thoughts, advice, and wishes? Arrange for any necessary duplication or printing and binding. In Appendix Two you will find several resources for printing.

5. Review/Renewal

If you choose to wait for a later presentation, it would be a good idea to make a schedule for reviewing your Ethical Will periodically. You may need or want to add to it or change the wording as your family conditions change. Some people become members by marrying into the family. Some are born into it. You may want to make some changes. After all, if you write to make a family member feel loved and included, but neglect to mention her "new" husband of three years, she might not appreciate his being ignored. She would not be mentioned by her new name or station in life. What about their new baby? By hurting her feelings, you could be thwarting your own well-intended efforts!

Which method will you use?

Additional ideas come from a published interview with Dr. Baines. He explains his **four** basic steps to create our ethical will.

The **first** is to make lists of ideas that you can apply to an outline.

The **second** is to write down your beliefs and opinions, some of your life choices, some of the insights you have gained, your most important values, etc.

The **third** idea for starting is to keep a journal or diary. You will gradually see a theme or main idea of your life emerge that you can explain for your children to understand.

The **last** idea is to get some professional help with the writing. A writer with experience in ethical wills will meet with you to let you express your values and thoughts concerning your ethical will.

The services of a *personal historian*, a professional

writer, could include brainstorming, editing, printing, ghostwriting, and/or audio or videotaping. It is a prudent idea to ask his or her experience in the field. Ask to see a sample of work. You can discuss methods of making a permanent version. S/he will provide you with assistance or with a finished document for your approval. The costs can vary widely, according to the hours spent and the services provided. It can run from, perhaps, $100 for an interview and a simple letter to many thousands of dollars for a lengthy, complicated, and comprehensive work.

If you have been making notes of things you need to mention, getting started will be easy. An outline can be blocked out, choosing three to five main topics that your ethical will should cover. These will probably be comprehensive and important (to you) concepts with titles like "My Marriages," "Who Needs a Formal Education?" "The Bright and Beautiful Pets in My Life," "My Long Road to Retirement," etc.

It is your book or letter. You can be as sophisticated or as corny as you like. This is a way to show your creative side to those grandchildren who seem to think you are a little bit stodgy!

What are you intending to put in the outline? The

ideas from your notes, probably, and an questions you pose to yourself. If you run low on just begin thinking of questions you would like to a your great-great grandmother. It would be an interesting conversation, because she never learned English, preferring her native German. Nevertheless, if you had questions for her, then your grandchildren probably have very similar questions for you. Just pretend they asked and begin your answers.

Building Your Confidence

You will build confidence in your writing simply by writing facts and descriptions. Later you will be ready to write your feelings. That is not so easy, sometimes. One trick to help you write more comfortably is to put the feeling within a sentence that is already begun. When you get to it, you may have thought about it subconsciously for more time than you realized.

For instance, make up some beginnings of sentences that you know you will be interested in addressing.

Examples might be:

I believe in...

The possession I value most is...

d to... because...

son was... because I learned...

ou got 'em or you don't, so you...

ethical behavior is not just for Sundays, but...

I always felt that my spouse would be...

I am so sorry that I ...

You would be surprised to learn ... about me.

It makes me very angry ...

It makes me very happy when...

"Feelings" can be a result of something you learned from experience. Gratitude is a feeling to be shared. Your political attitude and religious beliefs and social standing and appetite and color preference all are interesting points of view to those receiving your ethical will.

You might *surprise* those heirs who think they know you well *now* and you will *inform* those who will be born into your family *after you are gone*. If they are bored with it, they don't have to love it, do they? But be assured that almost everyone will enjoy interpreting your ethics and truths and tales.

Creativity

This example demonstrates *one way* that I get started. I simply write quickly and in general terms, making sure that I do not stop to rephrase or edit at all. The editing will come in one big undertaking after I have lived for a day or two with the ideas I have just written.

The following letter is an overview of an opinion or definition letter to my two sons. The bold face comments show what I will need to elaborate on. As I mention at the beginning, I will subsequently write a letter to each son, but this readily shows what is on my mind-- their relationships to the creative arts.

Dear Sons,

Each of you will have your own version of this note, but I will block out my ideas here first. I will write of many subjects before I finish these ethical will letters for you. Today my thoughts are on "creativity."

Creativity and the drive to create are very important to me. **Need to explain why.** My creativity has surfaced in many fields. I grew up and went to college thinking I had no artistic ability. In fact, had I known what I later learned about artistic ability, **Tell what I learned?** I would have majored in elementary art teaching. I just realized it too late.

I had to take private lessons to discover that I do

have some ability. During college I began to get the understanding from my friend Barb, an art major, that everyone has the capacity to create. But later, I took art lessons from another friend and found in myself a little talent. I worked hard to develop it and found some confidence, as well.

I allowed my creativity to flourish in Halloween costumes, birthday cakes, sewing, photography and many other things. **I should relate the activity to the creativity applied.** Finally, I allowed myself to venture into the realm of writing. I had always written, but only for myself. When I let myself show my work to others, I received compliments and interest.

Now I am pleased to acknowledge my creativity, and the purpose of this letter is to encourage you both to delve into your own abilities. Immerse yourselves! Jump right in!

D.G., you have terrific talent in art and in writing and some unmeasured ability in music. Keep using your interest and your talents. You have a fine ear for conversation. **Be generous with examples I remember.**

T.D., you have gift for clarifying ideas. While your brother devotes his imagination to novels of science fiction, you have an uncanny ability to define and promote ideas. Your college papers were outstanding. I think you probably still have some of the artistic ability you showed as a little boy. **What were some of the projects that seemed really good**? And I know you have a great singing voice that you so rarely let yourself exhibit. What about things you make with welding? After all, you trained and qualified as a welder before you chose your final majors.

Creativity can be demonstrated also in things like woodworking, cooking, and furniture arrangement.

This is weak; are there more manual arts to mention?

The production of something unique is so satisfying that I wish for both of you a life of creativity. Uncover your interest and abilities and allow yourself time to act.

Then leave some of your work for your children and grandchildren—in a recipe, photos, canvases, recordings, and notebooks. And share some of your creations with me before I am gone. I am your biggest fan!

Love,
Mom

NOTES

Chapter Six

When Should I Create my Ethical Will?

We will discuss just briefly the actual physical writing you will be doing. Whether you hit the computer, make a few notes with a pencil, or hire some professional help, you will be influenced by your own personality.

Larks and Owls

Did you know that in addition to being affected by your physical situation, you are also affected by the time of day? When you do your writing is affected by your own internal rhythms and preferences. You may be the most productive if you consider that there are two major types of work personalities, and they are nearly opposites--larks vs owls. It is mentioned because there is occasionally an individual who is totally frustrated by a writing "schedule." If s/he is trying to write after supper and gets too sleepy, perhaps the schedule should be changed to a half-hour session before breakfast every day.

If you are the early-bird, the lark, you may be inspired to work the first thing in the morning. You discover that the household is usually fairly quiet. Maybe your thinking is clearest then. It is possible that each evening you miss the end of the television show because you nod off. It becomes a situation in which your family sends you to bed to sleep after they wake you up. Yet somehow you amazing larks arise again at 5 a.m. or earlier. And you all just love to tell, in loud clear tones, that the sun is up and the day is wasting. It must be just as irritating when the owls say, "Oh! You are going to bed? So early?"

The folks who start slowly in the morning are, of course, the owls. They need to wake up slowly and warm up to their tasks. Once they clear their heads and get started, they do well. They just do it better later in the day or later in the night. Choose your best time of day and go to it. It isn't important when you write as long as you are writing.

Of course, no one can dictate when you will do your writing or where you will be able to work it in. Perhaps you have a job that takes you away from home each day. You may be able to sneak a short writing period into your busy day. Think about your free time, your time spent waiting for someone to arrive, or your time that is simply wasted when you sit waiting for appointments. These bits of time add up to quite a bit of time that could be used to write, or at least to make notes or to edit some recent work.

One excellent suggestion involves a small financial investment. If you buy a tape recorder or a digital recorder, you will be able to talk out your thoughts when your hands are occupied with some activity that precludes writing or typing. Later when you are able to get the ideas onto paper, you can listen to a sentence at a time. The new digital reorders can be set to play back the recording at a slower speed than it was dictated. There are also foot pedals that will control the playback as you write or type.

Retirees often say they are busier than ever. They might have to assign priorities to the ways they spend their time. Their ethical wills should be ranked near the top, because the writer is the only one who can do the writing and it is sad but true that none of us knows how much time we will have to do our writing.

Time gets away

Another concept of when to create your ethical will is when in your life experience do you begin writing ethical wills? That is entirely up to you and depends upon so many factors. Factors include things like your age, the ages of your friends and relatives, the circumstances, and perhaps their location. For instance, you might fire up your pen and write your old friend who has moved to Idaho, to complain to him about the raw deal he gave you in 1952 when you bought that old Ford truck from him. Remember—the one with the brake problem he didn't tell you about? If you are seriously asking for an apology, then get it sent while you are both in your right minds. And the same reasoning applies if you are kidding him about it.

Another example is the welcoming letter you write to your newborn grandchild. That should be written within a day or two while the wonder of the experience is fresh in your heart. Of course, it is never too late. Then it could be kept with your important papers until the child is old enough to read and value your gratitude and pride and thoughts. If you are around at the designated date of presentation (tenth birthday or whatever), you can give it to the child. But if you have gone on, what a treasure it would be for that child to realize that you loved him/her enough to plan ahead to give your love in a letter. The envelope could be dated so the administrator of your ethical will knows when to present it. (By the way, a law firm is more reliable to remember the right date than your favorite nephew is.)

Example:

Welcome, Newcomer

Dear Little Newcomer,

Welcome to our world, Harry! We are all delighted that you have come into our family. We have all been waiting for the day all the papers were signed and you would be with your new parents for good.

Who is this writing a letter to you? Well, my little brother grew up to be your mommy's dad. That makes him your grandpa, so I get to be your great aunt! But more important to you, I am just one of many relatives who were wishing your mom could someday be a mom. And now she has adopted you and you are her son.

You will be grateful, some day, that your birth mother knew that she loved you too much to let you suffer any problems when she couldn't do what was right for you. She gave you to Elizabeth so she could be your mom and love you.

Even though you will live far away from my house, I hope you will come to see me and play here. I would love to read books to you. I will look forward to your pictures and to hearing what you are doing in school, Cub Scouts, and sports. Your mother is a smart woman and she will do her best for you.

I know you will be good boy and a fine young man. Choose a good college and an interesting life. I hope I can get to know you better through the coming years. If I don't, you will have this letter to help you understand that I can love you very much no matter where we happen to be. And I always will.

Your Great-Aunt Marie

Would you like to write an ethical will letter to your son and daughter-in-law thanking them for that beautiful grandchild? They would love to receive your thoughts within the near future.

Example:

Praise for New Parents

Dear Douglas and Joan,

It may be difficult to see the keyboard as I begin this note to you both. I keep getting tears of joy in my eyes. It has been only two days since your long-awaited child was born. She is such a lovely little creature and such a quiet, good baby.

Thank you, thank you for making us grandparents. We are so grateful that you chose to have children and that you allowed us to join you in the birthing room. Having both parents and both grandmothers and a grandfather provides the opportunity to welcome a child with abundant love.

Joan, you are the star of this show. What a magnificent job you did propelling that baby into the world. No fuss, no complaint, just quiet hard work and a mother's love! I have tremendous respect for you. Even after a morning of hard work, you were in good spirits and were generous with your visiting time and in your allowing us to take all the pictures we wanted.

Doug, I know you were less than delighted to have so many people around for the event, but you were gracious and generous to allow us all into the room. It meant everything to us to see this first little granddaughter born and come into our lives. There are not words to adequately describe the feeling of seeing my own grown-up baby son at the moment he became the father of a baby daughter. I guess life is supposed to continue in just that manner, but it is a miracle to each of us each time it happens.

Now it is fun to see you learning all the little things that will be so easy for you within a few weeks. Changing diapers, giving a bath, playing but not playing too roughly, feeding her, and rocking her to sleep. You will enjoy it all once you gain your confidence. Before you realize that a year has gone by, she will be walking, then running, and saying a few words. One of them will be "Daddy."

Thank you for that wonderful day in our life and the promise for the future. With our love that continues to grow,

Mom and Dad

Another example is a heart-felt letter to your favorite aunt. Her influence upon you during your growing-up years was strong and you are grateful. If you are comfortable with her reading how you feel and acknowledging it and discussing it with you, then you would probably get it written and delivered. She is years older than you, so it is not unreasonable to expect her to die before you do. As they say, neither of you is getting any younger.

Example:

Appreciation Letter

Dear Aunt Rose,

Hello, my dear aunt! And how are you today? I think that you will be very surprised to receive a letter from me. You know that I have never been one to write much. But now I want to put some words on paper. I guess I would be a little too shy to say them face-to-face, but now that you know, maybe we can talk.

You wouldn't comprehend that, I realize. You have never, in all the years I have known you, been reluctant to say exactly what you thought in exactly the way you wanted to express yourself. I am grateful for the role model you have provided. You are very different from my mother, for instance, and that is good. It gives me alternate ways to behave and still be part of my society. It was enlightening for me to see a strong woman standing up for herself long before the women's movement entered our culture.

I have always been impressed by your generosity, Aunt Rose. When I was little, there was a Christmas present for me, and most years, you were the only relative who remembered my birthday. Thank you. That meant a lot to a little girl who was not warmly accepted by the rest of the family. You saw me as an innocent victim of a situation I had nothing to do with. If my father had married a different woman, I would have been the apple of my grandmother's eye. I cared a lot and it hurt when I was a kid. I can be honest with you; now I really don't care much what your mother or your sisters thought.

The last point I want to mention is the manner in which you are treating your husband as he sinks into the abyss of Alzheimer's Disease. It is remarkable how patient you have become. You never raise your voice to Uncle Roy, and you smile and listen to him telling a story to your guests for the fourth time in the same visit. It must be driving you crazy. He is such a fine man, as generous as you are, and he was a good businessman. He deserves better than to become a tragic/comic figure. You manage to treat him with respect and patience and love.

Your lovely sense of humor is getting you through most of the bad times. I am grateful you can see the humor in those awkward situations. Carry on, dear Aunt. I admire you and I love you.

Your niece,

The last point we need to concede in dealing with this idea of when to write your ethical will is that things happen that we never could have imagined and planned on. Strokes, other medical problems, accidents, and who knows what else, can occur and change everything. Something could happen to your intended recipient, or could happen to you and you might never finish your ideas for ethical wills. All you can plan on is yourself and your attitude today. Isn't it wise to do as soon as possible whatever is at the top of your list of priorities?

Narrative Psychology

So many people were so deeply disturbed by the events and consequences of the activities in our country September 11, 2001, that there was noticeable increase in internet interest in websites devoted to ethical wills. The shock of realizing that their family could be destroyed in a single moment compelled people to begin telling their families how they felt about them.

Many people had a change in their perceptions of family in relation to themselves, but they may have already had some serious changes they hadn't yet recognized. This book is not the place to go into it, but a new/old field of study seems to be (re)emerging in the discipline of Psychology. It is called Narrative Psychology, and as its name implies, deals with narrating or telling of stories, especially of one's own history. To all those skeptics who refused to accept the wild stories that grandpa told to entertain the grandchildren, we must concede that there *may* have been some justification of the skepticism. Flora writes in a summary of an article in *Psychology Today,* "You are more than the star and author of your own life story. You're also the spin master. How you tell your tale reveals whether you see yourself as victim or victor even when your story veers from the life you lived."

Psychologist Dan McAdams adds, "We are all tellers of tales, and we seek to provide our scattered and often confusing experiences with a sense of coherence by arranging the episodes of our lives. Starting in late adolescence, we manufacture our dramatic personal myths by arranging the episodes of our lives." Our optimism/pessimism begins in babyhood with the security and attachment we develop with others. The experimental stories we create in adolescence define our emotional work toward self-concept.

Since so many "first events" happen between ages 10 and 30, Rubin calls this time a "memory bump" and says it happens again to the elderly as they look back into their life experiences. An example is an experiment with college students in which they changed their "first memories" each year as they developed and matured. The 60-70-year-olds might select *one* to tell and retell.

It seems, then, that no matter what our life story has been, we have a tendency to rewrite it almost continually, and as we move from one period of life to the next, old memories may acquire a different level of importance. Does this make a difference in our acceptance of Great-Grandma's tale of the vicious spring blizzard and the orphan calf in the kitchen? No. Will it affect our acceptance of the idea of Great-Grandma as a six-year-old carrying a calf that is very heavy for her in from the north forty? Well, yes, but we can still enjoy the story and feel the desperation such families must have felt in their efforts to survive such conditions. We will trust that most of the stories are firmly based in fact and feelings, and are acceptable as family history. And the doubters are going to feel pretty silly when your great, great uncle confirms that his little sister did, indeed, help pull the sled after they found the freezing animal in the pasture on their way home from school.

You have heard our Midwestern joke, haven't you, about the many isolated, one-room schools out in the rural areas? The country school your granddad walked to, in blizzard or pouring rain, three miles from his home, uphill, both ways? By the way, the three mile part isn't a joke.

So take the wild stories as a form of entertainment, if you must, but be generous in understanding the storytellers as well as their stories. There is so much to be learned from them. At the very least, we can appreciate their desire to share with us and to give us their advice, as well. Do them the courtesy of listening, then think about it and take it or leave it.

Since writing your ethical will is a completely personal activity, any location where you prefer to write is acceptable. Some writers prefer a totally silent environment, while others like soft music playing in the background. Are you one of the writers who are happy to work in their pajamas for half the day? Or are you one who needs to get dressed to be ready for "work?"

Where should you work on your ethical will? Anywhere that you feel comfortable writing and thinking. Is there a spot where you have a good writing surface and a box or drawer for your tools? You will need paper, writing instruments, and maybe references such as a dictionary, a thesaurus, maps of the regions you will mention, and perhaps a grammar guide. Additional references might be portraits, snapshots, old letters, licenses and diplomas, diaries, autograph books, military papers, and other records.

Arrange your own writing space as you prefer it. If your living accommodations are too small for a desk, you might be able to use a lapboard or a clipboard or the kitchen table. If you have the luxury of a large house, you could set up a writing studio in a spare bedroom.

Despite all of your thoughtful consideration of location, you could find you just enjoy writing in the busy traffic through the living room. The best writing will be done when you are comfortable and in familiar surroundings.

You are lucky if you can sink into your soft, easy chair, because there are others of us who are far more effective sitting in a solid straight chair pulled up to a desk. But if you are creating your ethical will, enjoying the memories, and the sharing with your heirs, you probably will be comfortable even in a straight chair at the table.

Again, your ethical will is going to be a fairly

personal activity. If you want to share the ideas with your spouse, it can be pleasant to talk over what you are remembering and writing to your heirs. He or she can probably even be helpful to you by asking questions, if the concept is not quite clear. Fortunately or unfortunately, the questions that come up may trigger ideas of other things you want to say. I would strongly suggest that you begin a separate list of these new ideas, because they have an annoying way of slipping from our memory. You may use all of them or none of them, but at least you can make the decision if they are on a written list.

It is important to get right to your ethical will project. Frankly, we usually don't know just when we might be incapacitated. Rev. Thomas Owen-Toole adds,

> When you are dying, you aren't always in the best condition to share... There is also little assurance that our family or friends will be in good enough shape to hear what you struggle to say. Sometimes we are cogent during our closing days, but I wouldn't count on it.
>
> I'm quite conscious of the intentional or unintentional burdens, pressures and guilt we adults can implore upon our children, all in the name of loving advice. As we depart our earthly abode, our temptation is to get in our last licks, which is all the more reason to shape our ethical wills when we are far from the grave.

NOTES

Chapter Seven

When Do My Heirs Get to See It?

Wills are traditionally read after the demise of the writer. As we have explained, the ethical will is a little different. The traditional last will and testament carries out our intention of leaving our things of value to selected individuals or institutions. Some wills leave vast fortunes and are so complicated that it takes a whole office of lawyers and a judge to put it into effect.

In the ethical will, we carry out our intention of leaving our ethics and values to selected individuals. The ethical will can be just a line or two to reassure that the deceased wishes to be remembered and to assure the heir that s/he is remembered. Or it can be lengthy, complete, and even surprising to the heirs.

An Example of a light-hearted reminder:

To Whom It Might Amuse,

I leave to my son, Chuck L., my ability to laugh at anything. He shares that quality with me and we have had some wonderful sessions of belly laughing. True, it has gotten each of us into trouble at times, but the joy we share in laughing is deep. He can be trusted not to laugh unkindly at anyone. We just interpret hilarity where most people miss it.

Son, please remember me and laugh!

Love, Mom

The ethical will can be very serious, typical of the writer's personality, or light and fun, typical of the writer's personality.

Example of a somewhat serious approach to giving advice:

Serious Advice

To my son,

It occurs to me that I have never explained to you the reasons for which I have devoted myself, through donations of my time, effort, and ideas, as well as my considerable financial support, to the Republican Party in this state.

As you know, I come from a family deeply involved in farming. Most of my ancestors for several generations have toiled in the summer heat to raise and harvest hay and grains to feed the livestock that sustains the people of this country. My family has been known for honesty and fairness in business dealings. As farmers, we were small businessmen as surely as were the shopkeepers in town.

The GOP was for years the standard-bearer of this group of Americans. I joined the thousands of Midwestern farmers who believed in the politics and policies of the party. As little as fifteen years ago, I would have encouraged you to immerse yourself in the local political organization and offer assistance and financial support.

However, I hereby release you from any obligation to any political party. In case you might feel some pressure to spend your inheritance as you think I might have approved, I am letting you know that I am disgusted with both major parties and nearly all politicians. I think maybe the political groups that are promoting the green policies are encouraging the actions and attitudes that will save our earth and a decent standard of living. That decision will be up to you.

I would advise that you make your choices and decisions according to common sense and as much information as you can gather. Good luck finding the truth.

Your father

There is another excellent use of the ethical will. Consider it as a guide to the distribution of the many items among your personal effects that you would like to see in the hands of those relatives and friends chosen by you.

Traditional legal wills can designate which important items will go to the designated heir, but it is impractical to name the numerous small items that you know selected individuals would appreciate and enjoy.

What are some examples, you ask? Well, let's say that you have an ancient and well-used pocket knife that you have carried since you were nine years old. It has been helpful to you in hundreds of situations, from opening a can of beans on your first camping trip to cutting a switch to threaten your recalcitrant son when he let you know in some four-letter words that he would mow the lawn when he was good and ready. (He decided he was ready a moment later.) If none of your survivors knows that story, s/he wouldn't know it was not to be sold. It is difficult for a mourning spouse or relative to know the difference between some special item and the many other earthly goods we manage to collect.

How about using the knife as a starting place for an apology to that son? You know you wouldn't have switched him; not very hard, anyway. But does he know that? Shouldn't you tell him while you are able? Remember, an ethical will letter can accommodate two or three concepts. This example encompasses a personal apology and reinforces the ideas of respect for his mother and of thoughtfully sharing material treasures.

Example

Letter including an Apology

Dear Son,

This is the first page of a great many that I intend to write to you. There are a few hundred things I have been meaning to say to you before it is too late. Oh, don't worry. You don't have to respond or do anything about it; it is just stuff I should have talked about before.

Getting this first thing off my chest should make me feel better, no matter what your reaction is. It is just one of those things that I have had on my mind in the last year or so. I have been slowly coming to terms with my mortality, you might say. Before I go senile or get so weak I can no longer write this stuff, I had better just sit down and do it. Okay, here goes.

Do you remember that hot afternoon when you were supposed to mow the lawn and told me you weren't going to do it until you were good and ready? You were twelve years old and had been spending too much time with the neighbor boys. They were about 13 and 14 years old. They were a couple of spoiled, mouthy brats who were allowed to say what they pleased in words that would make a sailor blush. We should have known better than to let you play with them so much, but we didn't realize until too late just what they were like.

Anyway, your mother had company coming for ice tea and dessert that evening, so the mowing needed to be finished before supper. You told me you would do it when you got good and ready. And your language included words that you hadn't heard used in our house.

I took out my old pocketknife and stepped over to the hedge on the east side of the house and proceeded to cut a switch. I can't forget the horror in your eyes as you thought that your old man was going to hurt you. You had very rarely been spanked, and I doubt that I would have switched you for sassing me that day. I got lucky, though. You back-pedaled, saying you guessed if Mom wanted it ready for her company, you should get started. I want to apologize to you, anyway. It was not my usual way to discipline you and it frightened you. Can you forgive me?

By the way, the second reason for this note is this: I would like for you to have my old pocketknife when I am gone. Please keep it clean and sharp. The blade still holds a nice edge. If the thing is still of use in a few years, when Sean is a teenager, maybe he would like it as something from his old granddad. Teach him how to use the whetstone to put a keen edge on the knife and how to protect the edge as well as he can.

My eyes get tired so quickly these days, I guess I will quit for now and take this up again later. There is so much I want to tell you.

Dad

Some ethical will writers want to leave their advice, but cannot pull together enough thoughts on any one subject to organize their advice and opinions. The next letter is to all the five kids to take or leave as they care to. And this is all right, too, because slowly the love for his life and memories comes through this big man's scattered remarks.

This example is from a major book of personal history that I did with a client. Some names and places have been changed, but essentially, the father writes in his own style and in his own words the things he wants to explain about himself and his success.

Example of a stream of consciousness or rambling thoughts form.

My Philosophy

I set policies. I don't really tell anybody what to do. I'm not a micromanager. I just kind of set goals and explain what we want to do. I let people kind of run loose.

I always kept my word. If I told my employees I'd do something, they always knew that I would do it.

We always say that we weren't any smarter than anyone else, we just worked harder.

My philosophy on higher education and college degrees is that I don't think a degree is for everyone! A degree doesn't hurt and a degree probably helps open some doors, but practical common sense means more than anything else.

There are about four things in this world that contribute directly to success.

If you have common sense,

if you know how to get along with people,

if you are a self-starter, and

if you know how to work,

those things will probably bring you more success than any education will.

My son worked for a national company. He had been working in another smaller company that was bought out by the bigger company, so he was transferred into the home office. Each of the other home office employees had a college degree hanging behind his desk, but he didn't have a degree.

Now he is a manager with a national chain, and very high up. Some companies want that degree, and some companies want to hire you young and train you themselves. I'm not talking against education, because some people couldn't understand how I could teach and coach without a college degree. I have always been able to adapt. I guess my biggest asset is that I adapt to the challenge at hand.

I was once a building inspector. You know, that is because I've been around construction, not because I have any degrees.

I was first to arrange for adult apartment housing, which was unusual at the time. I did the first condominium adult housing project. That was a new concept we came up with.

I've always been able to adapt to new things. I don't know, really, but I think it is my common sense. A lot of the so-called entrepreneurs didn't have college degrees. Maybe years from now with technology involved, college will be necessary, but I don't think college is for everybody. I have a grandson who makes perhaps $80,000 a year as a lineman, and I think this country is going to need an increasing number of service people in the future.

I've always been a promoter. I've had good people under me. Like when I was a basketball coach, I needed to know just two main things. Number one, how to get the right people. And two, when you tell them something, they will do it. A lot of coaches baby-sit their players. Yet I had girls that I told to jump, and they would jump, and on the way up, they'd ask how high. They'd want to do it. So, it starts with recruiting.

Some of my better teams weren't made up of the *best* players. They were the *best working together in teamwork.* I had a lot of star players on most teams, but when you recruit players, you've got 12 kids who all think they should start.

I had a lot of businesses, mostly related to construction. I have liked construction all my life, and looking back, I can see how that philosophy helped me get my biggest project together. It was like grabbing a bear by the tail and not letting loose.

I should tell you that I had three good business friends who joined my team and we made a very effective team; a good banker, a good CPA, and a good attorney.

In my brief encounter with the academic world, I learned what a cliquish, foolish, jealous bunch of people they can be.

Going further with my philosophy, I have to say that I think teachers—and Lord knows we need them—have such tunnel vision! I am talking about the group as a whole. I think they know their profession, but they don't know their stand in the real world, most of them, anyway. No common sense.

Now, I'll talk about kids today. Educators have become so liberal that there is no backbone in education. I had a football coach so tough that if I missed a block, he'd backhand me and give me a bloody nose. We had no facemasks, and I learned. I have no problem with that. Some people have a problem.

Kids really want to know where they stand. I was in a hotel recently and this small boy was running around, up and down the hallway with the ice bucket, spilling ice all over the floor. His mother was standing right there, *right there watching him*. She kept saying, "No, Johnny." The kid paid no attention.

Finally, I said, "Doesn't he know what "no" means?"

I can think of a few more things to tell
my philosophy. I think there is nothing worse
lady smoking. But I never smoked, never d
never went into a liquor store. I never dressed
casually as to wear blue jeans, and I *never* ate
anything new. I don't know how old I was when I
decided not to eat anything I was not familiar with.

I don't ever remember drinking a glass of milk. If I
drink a glass now, I get sick. I don't know why. I
drink milk on cereal and I love ice cream; guess I'm
just different.

Borrowing money and being in debt never bothered
me. I was $400,000 in debt when I was 23. I was
buying houses and then more houses. I was in real
estate for a time and liked it. But I have always
learned to adapt to what I was doing.

One job I had was programming COBOL on a
computer as big as a car. I was totally engrossed in
my work, even forgetting to break for lunch until I
noticed that every other worker was gone. But after
I left that job, I never touched another computer. I
probably can still type, but my eyesight would be a
problem and I am a very poor speller.

That's the one thing I wish for that I haven't
earned or been given. My spelling is very elementary
and I have little knowledge of phonics or English. It
seemed like I was always busy with thoughts of new
ideas. I've always been creative, I guess. Some
people use the term "visionary."

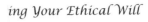
ny philosophy of life. I hope that
nake your life as successful as I

111

The following message cannot exactly be called a letter, but it is essentially a letter. It is borrowed from the actual writing by the father in a memory book I helped him and his wife make for their family. The father allows the classic poem about our children to speak for him. Then he elaborates on it by citing his own application.

Example

Short and Simple

This message is for all four of our children and their spouses,

From *The Prophet* by Kahlil Gilbran

And a woman who held a babe against her bosom said: Speak to us of children.

And he said: Your children are not your children.

They are the sons and daughters of Life's longing for itself.

They come through you but not from you.

And though they are with you yet they belong not to you.

You may give them your love but not your thoughts,

For they have their own thoughts.

You may house their bodies but not their souls.

For their souls dwell in the house of tomorrow, which you cannot visit,

Not even in your dreams.

You may strive to be like them but seek not to make them like you.

For life goes not backward nor tarries with yesterday.

You are the bows from which your children as living arrows are sent forth.

The archer sees the mark upon the path of the infinite, and He bends you with His might that His arrows may go swift and far.

Let your bending in the archer's hand be for gladness;

For even as He loves the arrow that flies, so He loves also the bow that is stable.

Sharon Foltz, our personal historian, helped us write our family history. Now she is urging us to try to put down some of the wisdom we have learned over the years. She calls it our ethical will, a way to leave you our sense of ethical behavior and our way of living. This is a little daunting but maybe there are some conclusions or observations we can make. We have included this piece from "The Prophet," which to some extent reflects our feelings about child raising. I think we have done fairly well to instill the widely accepted virtues of honesty, integrity, truth telling, compassion, and maybe frugality. Through permissiveness or ineptness, (you choose), we have left you pretty much to yourselves in the matter of religion, sexual matters, and politics. We think these are pretty much the techniques we learned from our parents. We probably can be criticized for lack of assertiveness and healthy dealing with confrontations but it seems to us you have mostly overcome that shortcoming in your upbringing. We have often spoken to each other how fortunate we are to have four families of children who have caused us such a minor amount of anxiety over the years and who are such great support to us while we are dealing with the infirmities of old age.

We love you all,

Dad and Mom

NOTES

NOTES

Chapter Eight

How Will I Write and Print My Ethical Will?

Handwritten notes

When you consider the many and various ways you communicate, this is perhaps the ideal time to devote the few extra minutes that handwritten papers require. The most important reason to write your will by hand is that you will be demonstrating a quality that is truly unique. No one else has the same handwriting, just as no one else has the same thoughts that you will be leaving to your loved ones. Recipients of your ethical will truly value it, both for the time you invested in your gift to them and for the sample of your individual handwriting style. If you happen to write a truly beautiful hand, it would be a real shame to deprive your heirs of the permanent example. The same goes for an unusual style--maybe you write quite small or print in all capitals or have an intense left-hand slant. Only the writer who is really handicapped by unreadable script should hesitate to put an ethical will in handwritten form. And finally, beautiful handwriting lends such dignity to a fine quality paper.

If you choose to write by hand, you will probably need to organize your thoughts and materials before beginning to write in order to avoid confusion. By outlining your thoughts or writing a rough draft, you can determine the best order of your ideas. I favor putting all the early work into a spiral notebook. All the pages stay together, but a page is easily torn out when you change your mind. A spiral is lightweight to handle and can go with you to appointments or activities where you might have some time to devote to your ethical will. You can work in some privacy in a waiting room, for instance, because most others waiting are reading or are preoccupied and probably will neither notice your writing nor distract you from it.

To help you choose a spiral notebook—I think the wide-lined is best no matter how large or small your handwriting. Limit your writing to only one side of the paper. Right-hand page or left-hand page as the spiral lies opened won't make any difference, but a left-hander might be more comfortable writing on the left-hand page, leaving the right-hand page blank.

Why restrict yourself to only one side? Because the pressure of the pen or pencil affects the surface of the second side, making it difficult to write on that back side and difficult to read the writing.

It is important that you leave at least two lines of space between the lines you write. It may seem like a waste of paper, but it is well worth it. The space allows easy corrections and additions. You may think of more details or names or ideas to make your ethical will more useful and interesting. With triple spacing, it is relatively easy to make the corrections.

Example: Typed with triple spacing and edited for spelling, usage, and accuracy.

Making corrections

Birthday celebrations have become far more

Sp?

elaborate and importtant to children than

they were in my day. It seems that every child

I know has had many birthday parties and

lots of presents every year.

When my brother and I were boys, we were

if we had a special dessert   acknowledgement

lucky ~~*to have a birthday cake*~~ *in* ~~*honor*~~ *of*

our birthdays. The best we got was a family

get-together for homemade ice cream and cake.

Our aunts and uncles, grandparents, and

cousins came to most of our family birthday

anniversaries because they were wonderful

opportunities

~~*excuse*~~ *to get together. I hope that today's*

overindulgence doesn't create a generation

of spoiled brats demanding recognition

existing another year!

just for ~~living until their next birthday.~~

Typed manuscripts

For many writers of the age group most interested in writing ethical wills, it is as natural as anything for them to choose the typewriter. That is fine. It is immoral, however, not to tell them about word processing programs. The word processor has made writing so much easier. An author can type a paragraph, change the wording, correct the spelling, and move the paragraph to another location within the article in a matter of seconds, never having printed a word of it. The article can then be saved to be added to or to be edited at a later time.

If the writer chooses to type his/her ethical will on a typewriter, it is important to triple space the lines for ease in corrections and additions. Again, it is easier to make the corrections and additions on a word processor. The cost of a basic computer/printer setup had been lowered drastically in the last few years. Some sales outlets offer instructional classes in using the computer. Some instruction can be in your own home.

Computers are now available in many public libraries for the patrons to use. Or perhaps you could borrow a computer and word processing program from a friend or family member.

Publishing/Printing Your Ethical Will

For our purposes we can use either the word publish or the word print. The will(s) will be, at least initially, for an individual or a very small group to read and appreciate. I take print to mean getting the words, photographs, drawings, maps, titles, bills of sale or lading, certificates, immigrations lists, letters, and any other documents you wish to include collected into a permanent form. That collection could be as simple as to be accompanied by a single handwritten copy of the ethical will written on tablet paper. Conversely, the collection could consist of photocopies of each piece of the related papers. The form you choose could also be a single (or a few) handwritten copy(ies) on the finest paper, hand-bound in a leather book. Or it could be a paperback book printed as a single copy or several hundred. The cost of a brief ethical will in the form of a single letter can be less than a dollar for paper and a pen. Costs of printing a booklet or book-length ethical will vary from less than ten dollars for a print-shop copy bound in an inexpensive cover to any amount you are prepared to spend.

Prices for book printing have come down to very reasonable rates for a type of paperback called "print on demand" printing. For an initial fee, a printing company can take your finished and edited manuscript, which you submit as a computer disk, and enter it into their master computer. Soon they are ready to print and send, within a matter of days, as many copies as you order. That order may be only one copy or many copies, but the cost per copy is the same. Cost of the books depends on their length and their physical dimensions. Some companies charge a little extra for color pages and for photographs. Most offer free or low-cost artistic help in designing a custom cover for your book.

It is an exciting time to become an author. By self-publishing your booklet or book, you will save the years it used to take to find a publisher and get into production and sales. Besides, the vast majority of ethical wills will be printed as single copies or in small numbers. Several print-on-demand and small-run publishing houses are listed in Appendix Three.

Other Formats for Ethical Wills

Recordings

It was mentioned in Chapter One that an ethical will may be created in a form other than a letter or a book. An audiotape of the wishes and thoughts one would like to leave his/her survivors would be cherished by the loved ones for whom it is recorded. Taping is relatively easy to a natural storyteller. Requirements include a good quality tape recorder and top quality tapes, a quiet environment in which to speak and record, and some organization of what you have already recorded. In the case of tape recordings, some experts suggest taping on only one side of the tape in order to avoid any confusion about order or content.   Labels should be attached immediately and the tape should be given a title and/or a number. The speakers should be identified. One method is for each speaker to announce, "I am giving this sample of my voice for voice recognition. I am John Q. Smith. This session of work on this ethical will is being recorded at my Uncle John Moral's home in Ethicsville, Iowa, on June 7, 2007."

If the session is being guided by questions from an interviewer, the interviewer should also provide an example of his/her voice. Many people using the audio method of leaving their ethical wills find it easy to talk smoothly and to the point if they are prompted by questions from another person. The questions can be planned ahead of time, but the resulting product may seem more like a portion of a memoir or part of a lifestory project.

One of the major points of leaving an ethical will is to make it a private sharing of one's thoughts and wishes and hopes and advice for the receiver. If a family member leads the session by asking questions, the ethical will loses some of that privacy. If the interviewer is a person unknown to the recipient, it may seem less focused and personal. A professional personal historian may be better suited to the task because s/he will shift the emphasis to the "answers." In fact, the personal historian will more likely mention a subject briefly and then keep quiet as the creator of the ethical will speaks on the subject, saying exactly what s/he intended to tell the will's recipient.

Tape recordings can duplicate the sound of the speaker's voice so accurately that it brings tears to hear them. If one is unable to organize the writing of ethical wills, tape recordings can be an alternative. If time is of the essence, taped sessions can be done with relative speed. Later, if it is desired, the tapes can be transcribed to paper to be enjoyed through reading. A caution about taped ethical wills: Tape recordings are not forever. They can easily be damaged by heat or magnetic fields.

Digital Recording

A newer type of recorder does not employ tapes. It is called a digital recorder, since sound is converted to a form recognized and stored digitally. The sound is said to be superior and less subject to distortions. It is less likely that the recordings will be harmed or destroyed, but it is always possible that they could be accidentally recorded over.

CDs and DVDS

There is a present-day solution to that problem, of course. Tape recordings and digital recordings can be rerecorded onto computer disks, either CDs or DVDs or who knows how many other forms by the time this book reaches you! The disks are subject to some dangers of magnetism, etc., but they are proving to be more stable than the common recording tapes. In addition, they don't stretch and distort the sound if they are paused too often, and they don't get tangled on the capstan and break.

Photo albums and photo essays

What about using a photo album as the basis for an ethical will? It could be a family album, of course, but consider other possibilities. Have you been a Sunday School teacher for more years than you can remember? Are there collections of photos and printed programs from the numerous church suppers, Bible Schools, reunions of couples married in your church, and missionaries and other visitors? You may find that you are one of very few who can remember much about those occasions. You should probably be making notes of what you recall of the occasions and about the many people who were instrumental in them. Then you could organize and leave that information as your ethical will to your beloved church. It is perfectly proper for you to commend the many church workers and volunteers, encouraging their continued participation and contributions. It is fine for you to include a statement of support and your wishes for the future activities of the church.

Your ethical will is your opportunity to express yourself. Your words and wishes could live on for years and influence things more than you ever had hoped. After you are gone, the will could be read to the congregation or just the board of directors, or the

Sunday School, or at the luncheon served after your funeral, or at the Memorial Day Picnic, or whenever and to whomever you wish.

It is also possible for you to share the ethical will you write for your church friends while you are still living, but that could bring up new and confusing problems for you. You could suffer a backlash brought about by jealousy. Too many people might call you to thank you or just to discuss such a concept as your ethical will. The whole activity might upset or frighten some friends who jump to the conclusion that you are expecting to die soon. That could be ironically funny if you subsequently spent all your Sundays for the next thirty years right there in the congregation where you have been for the last fifty years!

And our final ideas for communicating with your ethical will heirs—try some poetry, or maybe just some truly beautiful passages from the classics or the Bible. Give credit where credit is due and change the wording to suit your situation. Especially in music, you can substitute words or phrases and convey a strong message to your heirs. Just don't let it get into the commercial world of music or you will have to pay royalties.

To reiterate our theme...it is up to you how you do it, but it is important to get busy with some activities to begin your ethical wills. Good intentions never get handed down to the next generations. Are you going to take your good intentions with you, or will you try to share your thoughts while you are still able?

"I have not encountered one person yet who hasn't told me that the level of peace of mind that they achieved by writing this is just amazing. They talk about a burden being lifted from their shoulders," said Dr. Baines (2002), thinking of his experiences at the hospice.

Dr. Rachael Freed, (2003) a therapist and social worker who has gained experience with ethical wills by conducting workshops, has written her own book about ethical wills from the feminist viewpoint. She said, "People come away from this process with a lot of appreciation for their life, a lot of gratitude for the blessings in their life, and--maybe most importantly-- that they have something to give."

Sharing the good and the questionable

How about an amusing poem or a silly song to say some of the things you are feeling and want to share?

That works for some folks. Of course, you will avoid items of questionable taste and language.

I wrote this silly little attention-getter in about an hour. This whole book is based on a serious theme, so relax for a moment and enjoy this small joke, just for fun.

Example

DOGGEREL DIRECTIONS

OR

A LIGHTHEARTED LOOK AT THE ETHICAL WILL

DEAR SON OR DAUGHTER, AS THE CASE MAY BE,
MAKE YOURSELF COMFY; I'LL GET YOU SOME TEA.

I'VE ASKED YOU HERE TO SHARE MY LETTER
KNOWING YOUR LIFE CAN TURN OUT BETTER.

I HAVE LIVED MANY YEARS ON THIS OLD EARTH:
MORE THAN SIXTY HAVE PASSED SINCE MY HUMBLE BIRTH.

BUT I, TOO, SHALL SOME DAY GIVE UP THE GHOST,
BUT NOT WITHOUT TELLING WHAT I VALUE MOST.

YOU THINK YOU DON'T CARE AND THAT I WASTE YOUR TIME,
BUT THE REAL WASTE IS MAKING THIS DARN POEM RHYME!

IF IT GETS YOUR ATTENTION, IF IT MAKES YOU THINK,
THEN I HAVE SUCCEEDED IN FORGING A LINK

FROM PARENT TO CHILD AND TO CHILD AGAIN.
WE PASS ON THE VALUES THAT MAKE US FINE MEN.

VALUES LIKE GRATITUDE, LOYALTY, LOVE,
HONESTY, AND HARD WORK THAT PUT US ABOVE

THE LAZY, THE LIARS, THE ONES WHO WON'T TRY,
AND THE ONES WHO REPEATEDLY JUST SLIDE BY.

THEY DON'T TELL THE TRUTH, OR LOOK IN YOUR EYE,
THEY MAKE YOU FEEL NERVOUS, THOUGH YOU DON'T
KNOW WHY.

I VALUE THE COURAGE THAT MAKES A BOY TRY
TO BE LIKE HIS FATHER—A REGULAR GUY.

A GOOD HUSBAND AND FATHER, A GOOD SON, TOO,
AND ABOVE ALL, A MAN WHOSE WORD IS TRUE.

I VALUE THE STRENGTH OF THE TEENAGE GIRL
WHO LISTENS TO MOM 'BOUT THE SOCIAL WHIRL.

SHE'S ATTRACTIVE, SHE'S FUN, AND THINKS SHE'S READY,
BUT MOM SAYS ONCE MORE TO ACT LIKE A LADY.

THE WISE DAUGHTER LISTENS AND TRIES TO PRESENT
HER BEST BEHAVIOR WITH NO ARGUMENT.

BUT ARGUING'S FINE, IF THERE'S REAL GIVE AND TAKE.
IT IS CLOSED-MINDED PEOPLE WHO NEVER CAN MAKE

A CAREFUL DECISION BECAUSE THEY DON'T CARE
AND THEY WON'T EVEN TRY TO BE THOUGHTFUL OR FAIR.

ARE YOU GETTING THE GIST OF MY LETTER, MY CHILD?
MY VALUES ARE CULTURED, BUT MY POETRY'S WILD!

I CAN'T HELP IT, YOU SEE, IT'S A CURSE OF SOME KIND.
I WRITE THESE DUMB COUPLETS JUST TO UNWIND.

I MUST CEASE AND DESIST, FOR YOUR SANITY.
TO GO ON WOULD ONLY SHOW CRASS VANITY.

I KNOW THIS DOGGEREL IS TRASHCAN-BOUND
BUT THE VALUES IT HIGHLIGHTS ARE TRULY SOUND.

SO HOLD TO YOUR VALUES, TO YOUR OWN SELF BE TRUE,
AND <u>THINK</u> JUST A LITTLE, ABOUT WHAT <u>YOU'LL</u> DO!

More ways to share

We have mentioned writing, both letters and books, but what about writing a few stories that you feel are good teaching methods for recipients who might not accept straight advice? You know who they are. That hardheaded nephew of yours who was born knowing it all. No one has been able to tell him anything since the day he discovered his mouth. Many have tried to reach him, but he refuses to acknowledge that he could be mistaken. Let's make an ethical will for him. At least he can read, we think.

Example

Advising through stories

Dear Nicky,

These are my thoughts for you as I enter the last few months of my life on earth. I don't have a lot of time left to straighten out the world or even my fun-loving nephew. After I am gone, you will be given this letter. Read it and think about it. Please keep the letter to look at again when you are ten years more mature.

My wonderful sister has given you life and a great childhood and has exhibited more patience with your behavior than I ever thought she could muster. Why so patient? Because she and your dad love you more than anything. Hell, Kid, everyone in this family loves you. If I didn't love you and feel you have the ability to make yourself a good life, I wouldn't be spending my remaining time hoping to give you a few ideas for improving your situation. I will limit my lecture to a page or two. Here goes...

Nick, when are you going to stop looking out for only yourself and your friends and expend a little energy and interest in growing up? I know that lecturing won't bring about any change in your attitude.

How do I know? I have walked the walk and talked the talk because I heard the same talk when I was a little younger than you are now. I learned a serious lesson that I have told to only two other people. Ever.

It was the spring of the year I was 18, a senior in high school, barely passing in a general track of courses. I had been going with a girl for a few months when it began to dawn on me that we got along very well and that she was rather pretty and that I could enjoy a life with her. We went together for four more months and things got even better. She was entirely dependable. She was a hard worker and her mother had taught her to be a great housekeeper. She could cook everything I loved and was generous in finding time to cook for me. I enjoyed her company and even put up with her family on many nights when I didn't have the money to take her out. I was involved in fixing up my car and it seemed to eat every cent I could earn. My job wasn't great and I couldn't tolerate putting in overtime when all my friends were out driving around and having fun. Like you, I didn't have any interest in college, so why burn my brain studying stuff I would never use anyway?

If I was late getting to her house, she would always have a plate of supper saved for me. She never complained when it was too late for a movie or to go skating or do whatever our plans had been. Life was good, so on her birthday, I mentioned to her that when we got married we would start saving for a newer car. She laughed and made a smart remark that that car wasn't even on the drawing boards yet. She asked how much money I had saved right then. I had to tell her that I had no savings. She asked what I was going to do to earn enough to support a wife and family. I said I would find something better after school was out for the summer. She turned down the volume on the new car radio she had given me for my birthday two months earlier. Then she asked coyly, "What did you choose for *my* birthday?"

I stammered that I was proposing to her and her gift would be a diamond ring that she and I would pick out and buy on installments. We would go tomorrow to a jewelry store in the mall. Then she asked quietly if I loved her.

That conversation was getting out of control. My control. I couldn't get any serious words out to give her an answer. I tried to change the subject, to lighten up, as they say these days. She had the bit in her teeth, though, and wasn't slowing down. She let me have it. Must have been saving up her anger for a long time. Nicky, her words still echo in my empty brain. She stayed calm and used a low, quiet voice that hurt me more than screaming at me would have. She stated that marriage was for adults and I wouldn't qualify for some time to come. If I were still interested in her after I had finished high school and college and if she were available, she might be interested in beginning a relationship again.

We ended it that night. I spent a lonely summer. The day after graduation, my parents told me I had that I could live at home free for that summer and that I would work full time somewhere to help with college costs. They made me save 75% of my earnings! If I was accepted at a college, my money would go for transportation and clothes. If I could not or chose not to go to college, the money would pay for my own apartment.

Since I didn't have much time or money to spend on my car, I sold it. I sulked for a week in June. Finally I got a better job and tried to grow up a little. I rode a bicycle all over town and began to enjoy it. With no car, I dropped out of the gang I had been running with and found a couple of nice guys at the library when I stopped in to borrow a bicycle repair manual. Don't laugh. They are still friends of mine all these years later. They talked me into going to their small college.

It was tough and I still missed my girl. But I learned to study, to quit procrastinating, and to try to see another's point of view. Those three things would take you a long way toward growing up, Nick. They would enable you to learn the things that will help you get a better life, and it would give your parents a break. The things they say to you do have a great deal of merit. Remember, they are on your side. I hope you will listen and be able to agree with them somewhat while there is still time to avoid the serious legal troubles you have been flirting with.

I did finally get over the girl. It helped when I went to her house after college graduation, just to say hello, and she introduced me to her husband and baby daughter. So much for waiting. Well, she didn't say she would wait, and I can't blame her. I had been a self-centered, selfish child when she told me off.

Anyway that freed me to play the field. Because of my education, I was earning a lot of money and I had learned to manage it well. Within a year I met the young woman who eventually became your aunt. Where? At the same library; she was working there part time. I had grown up and was ready by that time to begin the life I wanted with this lovely woman. The life *we* wanted, with a family and our own home, and even a nice car. We went one step at a time and managed carefully.

Nicky, I could have retired eight years go if I had wanted, but I was happy working at my job. Now I am retiring to spend this precious time with my family. You are a part of the family and I sincerely hope you will find the path to your own happiness. Please don't insist on being right in every conversation. Just be productive and take better care of yourself. Selfishness and immaturity are not pleasant things to watch. Your parents deserve better from a great kid like you could be and possibly will be. I'm betting on you. I love you, nephew. Goodbye.

Your old Uncle Roger

Uncle Roger led quite the life as a young man, didn't he? And in all these years, he hasn't felt he could talk about it much. Perhaps it went against his current social status and standard of living. Yet when he generously decided to tell young Nick to mend his ways, he elected to show him by example. Their personalities were so similar. Roger may not live long enough to see a change in Nick, but he feels so much better and greatly relieved, just knowing that he tried.

The examples in this book, as I said in the introduction, were not intended to be copied word for word. I tried to step into the shoes of several types people as I of wrote some the ethical wills and then I borrowed a few from which I thought we could learn. You have learned that ethical wills are sometimes hard work, and sometimes frustrating, but even those concepts serve two very important values. They show the tangible products resulting from your hard work and they show the value of perseverance. They bring forth much appreciation for your thoughts and your kindness, no matter how much frustration you have hidden behind that piece of paper.

It will be worth every moment of effort when you see the gratitude and happiness in the eyes of your intended heir. It is enough to make you very glad you applied a little of that love you are leaving him or her just to see him holding your ethical will in their hands, appreciating it and planning to keep it always.

But please keep in mind that if you are a little shy about saying what you think, your ethical will can be more comprehensive and honest if you choose to leave your ethical wills to be opened after your death. If you choose that method, then you know you have offered your thoughts and perhaps some good advice, even though you might not know how it was received and acted upon.

If you glance back through the book, you will notice some white space before new chapters. That space is there for you to write in, making notes. If you jot down the names of people involved, the approximate year and part of the country it took place, and the point of the story, you probably will recall later the reason you wanted to write it. Memory is tricky and fickle, but notes last as long as we know where we left them and know how to use them. If reading examples of the work of others helps you, pleases go on to Appendix One.

I am leaving you my encouragement and my wish for pleasant memories and associations resulting from your ethical wills.

NOTES

NOTES

Appendix One

More Examples of Ethical Wills

Example

A letter to all my children,

At this stage of my life, it's seems prudent to put some of my thoughts on paper before I become unable to remember them, unable to express them, or am beyond the point of caring. My thoughts are mostly of you children. You have been my life since before the first one was born. Nothing in this world is more important than your father and you children--my family.

Much of the time, my thoughts take the form of a wish for each of you to be happy in your accomplishments. You each have your own dreams. Never give up on them, and try to be happy along the way.

I've always wanted only the best for you even though at times it didn't seem that way to you. I have made so many mistakes, but honestly, I was doing the best I could. It is important now that I ask your forgiveness and understanding of those mistakes. I don't know why I was so blessed to have you kids. I didn't deserve such happiness. I am so grateful.

Now we are beginning to see the next generation. I am so very pleased and grateful to have seen at least the first grandchild. She is adorable, of course. I know the Bible says, "be not proud," but I have to admit I'm a proud mom and grandma. I love watching you interact with her. You are doing such a fine job. She demonstrates such great love because she knows she is so loved. She demonstrates such intelligence because her parents are so intelligent and patient and thoughtful. And yes, she is truly beautiful, as all children are, but try to remember that kind of beauty is only skin deep. Her sparkle and responsiveness and good behavior are her real beauty. If there are more grandchildren in the future that I cannot meet, please tell each of them that I was waiting for them, but I had to go on. I will know them later.

We have such family memories, don't we? A lifetime full. And of course, we have a few regrets, too. Well, life isn't always fair, so we accept what comes and do the best we can. Then we try to make it better, more acceptable, and never look back with regret, just in our various forms of nostalgia.

I hope each of you can relax and see the beauty of the simple things in life and the joy in everything. And never lose your sense of humor. Never. As I am very much aware, time gets away from us so easily. Try to make the most of every day, every moment.

This advice is just the beginning. The longer I live, the more you are in for! I will pull out this ethical will every few months and add to it until I have spewed out all the ethics and advice I think I should pass along.

Know now and always that I love you all so very, very much.

All for now,
Mom

Example

Confession

This example is totally fabricated. It represents one chapter in a rather lengthy ethical will written by a widowed father of two. At the time of this writing, J.J. (John J. Jr.) is 30 years old and Janie is 28.

Chapter Four

Please Forgive Me

This chapter it is going to be difficult to write. I only go into the details because I am asking your forgiveness. When I had to face my alcoholism, I had to acknowledge the great deal of assistance I had in facing my illness. So many people were patient with me and helped me along the way. I have thanked a few of them but never you two.

Janie, you don't remember this because you were only three and a half years old when I quit drinking. J.J. says he remembers vaguely some of the arguments and trouble in the family when he was five. I am sorry it made an impression.

Bear with me; the story isn't too long. It happened on a Sunday afternoon. In A.A. they call it an intervention.

We were living in that small trailer home. I can remember the details of the story because I was fairly sober. I had suffered the flu for most of the week and had not been drinking. J.J. and two older cousins had been banished to the yard to play. Janie was down for her nap. It was really crowded by the time my two sisters and two brothers and my mother and my in-laws and my wife collected in the living room to tell me what they thought. To make a long story short, they told me I was drinking too much and failing my family. I had betrayed them, embarrassed them, and cost them time and money.

As the last tearful words of my wife faded away, a great quiet settled over the room. I knew I should answer, but I couldn't think of a thing to say. I couldn't quite believe what I had heard. I looked at each confronting member of my family and then I looked through the open doorway into the tiny room you kids shared. I saw my little blonde daughter, only three and a half, sitting in her crib on her knees, her chin on her hands on the rail, just looking at me. Then shattering the quiet of the room came this little voice: "And another thing, Daddy...YOU STINK!"

My mother-in-law gasped and muttered, "From the mouths of babes..." Then for some unfathomable reason my wife got the giggles. It wasn't funny, of course. It was probably a reaction to the tension. But soon everyone in the room was laughing, except for me. It wasn't funny to me and it wasn't easy but I stopped drinking that day.

The next time you kids helped me with my problem was the spring that J.J. was a senior in high school. The day he turned 18 was a Friday and he had come home tired from a track meet. After a nice birthday meal in the evening, I took him with me to our neighbor's back yard where several guys were having a beer and talking. I guess I was thinking to initiate him into adulthood or something. When we arrived my neighbor handed me an icy cold soft drink, then hesitated. He offered me a beer with one hand and a soft drink with the other, nodding his head toward J.J. I smiled and took the beer. I handed it to J.J., who answered, "No thanks, Dad. I'm in training. Besides, that stuff will kill you. I don't think I ever will drink." I thought that was a pretty bold statement for a young man to make in front of the guys. I was pretty proud of him.

I haven't had a drink in nearly 25 years, but a cold beer still looks good on a summer evening. You kids can live without it, and as you saw as you grew up, life is much less complicated without the alcohol. That's all of the advice I will give you on that subject.

Example

A Set of Principles for Living

This ethical will is taken from the book *called Ethical Wills: Putting your values on paper* by Barry K. Baines, MD. from Appendix 1, p. 96-98. It is written by Michael Greenspan, and I think it will become a classic in ethical will examples.

Having disposed of my property through duly executed documents, I now turn to the harder job of leaving to my children, Lisa and David, a set of principles that they should consider in living their own lives and helping to shape the lives of their children.

1. Do the right thing--as often as you can.

2. Only worry about those things that you can do something about.

3. Try as hard as you can, and, having done so, don't look back if things don't work out.

4. Work hard, but stop before you mindlessly began work to ask whether you have found the most efficient thing to work hard at.

5. You are not the center of the universe. If it takes religion to make you realize that, then embrace religion.

6. Happiness is NOT what feels good at the moment. You also have to consider the long-term consequences of your actions as well.

7. Be positive; try to find the best in a bad situation.

8. Be interested in a lot of things. People who are interested are interesting.

9. Show everyone you love that you love him or her, and be sure to tell him or her as well.

10. Divide the world into two groups: those that are trying to hurt you and those that aren't. Fight the first group as hard as you can and cut the second group as much slack as you can.

11. In making decisions, tend toward those that maximize your options.

12. Procrastinating over a decision until there is no decision to be made is itself a decision.

13. The best trait, in a friend, co-worker, or yourself, is dependability. The second is loyalty.

14. If you find a good, true friend, hold on to him or her as hard as you can.

15. Ask not what people do, but how well they do it.

16. Be fruitful and multiply.

17. And three that I have heard before but really like:

    a. When things are going REALLY wrong, remember: that which doesn't kill you makes you stronger,

    b. Love like you've never been hurt before, and

    c. Dance like no one's watching.

Example

Please forgive me, if you can

Dear John,

Well, I guess I have mellowed in my old age. I'll be 55 next week, and considered a senior citizen in some circles. But I've always tried to avoid running in circles.

Why am I writing to you now? I know it has been several years since we talked. I remember it well because I met your wife (I want to say new wife, although the two of you have had more anniversaries than you and I ever did,) and your youngest child. By the way, your daughter looks a lot like you did in your junior high years.

Now I am writing to let you know that I have matured enough to be able to say, "I'm sorry." Took me long enough, didn't it? Could you find it in your heart to forgive me, someday?

I am sorry I didn't believe enough in us. I am sorry for letting myself be influenced as I was by the stupid media frenzy at the time. Now I know it was partly well-intended by those honestly believing and encouraging women to be independent, and partly a grand scheme to sell newspapers, magazines, and books. I bought my share of books, and I swallowed a lot of the bologna they were serving.

When I split, I really thought we would both be better off. Were we?

I know I hurt you very deeply and you didn't deserve it. We had our share of little arguments, but it should have been a better marriage than it was.

I must take the blame. I expected you to change and demonstrate some of the new American attitude. But you hadn't read what I had, heard what I heard at college—in class as well as extra-curricular--or been confused by the feminists' bid for power.

Those were strange times. Looking back with clearer eyes than I had then, I can see that we had the American dream. We *were kids together, went through school together, and should have had the same goals for the future.*

But I messed up. I changed in ways you wouldn't or couldn't understand and could never have followed, anyway.

The point of this letter is not to stir up anything or to cause any upsets. I just needed to say I was wrong and that I am sorry.

You recovered and created a good, solid marriage and family and I am glad.

Still love you, always will.

Me

We Will Not See Each Other Again...

In 1854, a young man was leaving Germany to go to the United States. His father, knowing he couldn't protect his son, gave him the next best thing he could—good solid advice on how to live his life. The following two paragraphs are part of his ethical will to his son:

> It is doubtful whether we shall see each other again in life; and from afar I cannot warn you against such dangers as often threaten youth. Yet even from the furthermost distance, I shall think of you only with fatherly love and will at all times do everything in my power to help you...

Always seek to keep you conscience clear, i.e.. Never commit an action which you will have to regret afterward. Think carefully about everything you contemplate doing before its execution, and consider its consequences, so that you will act only after due consideration. A sure test of a clear conscience is an unclouded temperament and a cheerful spirit. Since you have received both from nature, seek to preserve them... (Schulman)

Sam Levinson's Unpaid Debts

Sam Levinson was an American humorist on TV for a time. He published the following in 1976.

"'Ethical Will and Testament to My Grandchildren and to Children Everywhere"

I leave you my unpaid debts. They are my greatest assets. Everything I am—I owe.

1. To America I owe a debt for the opportunity it gave me to be free and to be me.

2. To my parents I owe America. They gave it to me and I leave it to you. Take good care of it.

3. To the biblical tradition I owe the belief that man does not lives by bread alone, nor does he live alone at all. This is also the democratic tradition. Preserve it.

4. To the 6 million of my people and to the 30 million other humans who died because of man's inhumanity to man, I owe a vow that it must never happen again.

5. I leave you not everything I never had, but everything I had in my lifetime: a good family, respect

for learning, compassion for my fellow man, and some four letter words for all occasions: words like help, give, care, feel, and love.

.... Finally, I leave you the years I should like to have lived so that I might possibly see whether your generation will bring more love and peace to the world than ours did. I not only hope that you will, I pray that you will. (Schulman)

Reprinted by permission of Sterling Lord Literistic, Inc.
© by Sam Levinson, 1977.

These Things I Wish for You

This nice ethical will has been circulating through the internet, sent from one friend to another. It is attributed to radio personality Paul Harvey. Harvey did read the essay in 1997 on his radio program, but he did not actually write it. Its original title was "These Things I Wish for You," The author was Lee Pitts. It had been altered into many forms before it was read by Harvey. But it sounds to most of his listeners very much like a Harvey essay.

It doesn't matter, for our purpose of offering the example, who wrote the piece. I agree with the tone and the sense of nostalgia it gives us. A writer of an ethical will could piggyback on some of these ideas without actually plagiarizing the work. Just change the examples and keep the sentiment.

These Things I Wish for You

Lee Pitts

We tried so hard to make things better for our kids that we made them worse. For my grandchildren, I'd like better.

I'd really like for them to know about hand-me-down clothes and homemade ice cream and leftover meat loaf sandwiches. I really would.

I hope you learn humility by being humiliated, and that you learn honesty by being cheated.

I hope you learn to make your own bed and mow the lawn and wash the car.

And I really hope nobody gives you a brand new car when you are sixteen.

It will be good if at least one time you can see puppies born and your old dog put to sleep.

I hope you get a black eye fighting for something you believe in.

I hope you have to share a bedroom with your younger

brother/sister. And it's all right if you have to draw a line down the middle of the room, but when he wants to crawl under the covers with you because he's scared, I hope you let him.

When you want to see a movie and your little brother/sister wants to tag along, I hope you'll let him/her.

I hope you have to walk uphill to school with your friends and that you live in a town where you can do it safely.

On rainy days when you have to catch a ride, I hope you don't ask your driver to drop you two blocks away so you won't be seen riding with someone as uncool as your mom.

If you want a slingshot, I hope your Dad teaches you how to make one instead of buying one.

I hope you learn to dig in the dirt and read books.

When you learn to use computers, I hope you also learn to add and subtract in your head.

I hope you get teased by your friends when you have your first crush on a boy/girl, and when you talk back to your mother that you learn what Ivory Soap tastes like.

May you skin your knee climbing a mountain, burn your hand on a stove, and stick your tongue on a frozen flagpole.

I don't care if you try a beer once, but I hope you don't like it. And if a friend offers you dope or a joint, I hope you realize he is not your friend.

I sure hope you make time to sit on a porch with your Grandma and/or Grandpa and go fishing with your Uncle.

May you feel sorrow at a funeral and joy during the holidays.

I hope your mother punishes you when you throw a baseball through your neighbor's window and that she hugs you and kisses you at Hanukah/Christmas time when you give her a plaster mold of your hand.

These things I wish for you - tough times and disappointment, hard work and happiness. To me, it's the only way to appreciate life.

Appendix Two

Useful Terms and Phrases

While the term Ethical Wills seems to be gaining in popularity and will probably be established as the standard name, I have come across several appropriate terms that have also been used. If one of them appeals to you, you may certainly substitute the name.

Alternate names for Ethical Wills

Ethical Legacy
Eternal Values
Donor Legacy Statement
Heritage Values Expression
Legacy Continuum
Legacy Letter
Legacy Planning
Legacy Statement
Life Values
Living Values
Values Statement

Ethical Wills Word List

The following words and phrases might help you decide what you would like to cover in your ethical will. They could be inserted easily into an outline of the things you want to remember to say, or you could make notes as you think of them. See the two examples below.

Achievements—*scholarly, business, weight loss,*

Adoption

Advice

Ambition—*good- Harry's plans; bad-his wife's greed*

Aspirations

Balance

Birth

Blame

Blessed

Celebrations

Cherished

Church

College

Common sense

Competition
Conservation
Conservative
Cook
Cooperation
County Assistance
Creation
Crossed over
Death
Defeat
Development
Direction
Discipline
    Backtalk
    Grounded
    Lenient
    Punishment
    Strict
    Thrashing
    Whipping
Dreams
Dying
Economy
Education
Efficiency

Emancipated

Evil

Family

    Ancestors

    Grandparents

    Parents

    Brothers, sisters

    Sons, daughters

    Grandchildren

    Stepchildren

    Foster children

    Heirs

Family secrets

Family tree

Fears

Free

Freedom

Friends

Generation

Giving and receiving

Golden Rule

Good intentions

Graduate

Gratitude

Growth

Guidance

Home

Honesty

Honor/dishonor

Hypocritical

Inspirations

Insurance

Justice, fair play

Liberal

Love

Marriage

Manners

Memories

Military service

Mission

Money

    Big spender

    Credit Cards

    Debit Cards

    Enforced savings

    Earning a living

    Financial Planning

    Income

    Interest

    Investments

Principal

Taxes

Wages

Morals

Motivation

Named for

Natural

Old

Older people

Old saying

Old ways

Opportunity

Ought to

Passion

Persistent

Perseverance

Personal

Pets

Politics

Pregnancy

Pride

Protect

Proud

Proverbs

Public-service

Question

Recognition

Relationships

Relatives

Reflections

Religious

Respect

Responsibility

Revenge

Reward

Risk

Sacrifice

Self discipline

Senior citizen

Sincerity

Spiritual

Storyteller

Sports

Sunday school

Team work

Thoughts

Travel and transportation

    Horse and buggy

    Luxury cars

    Model T

Muscle cars

Space travel

Train travel

Truth

Waste

Workman

Wallflower

War

World War I, II

Korean Conflict

Vietnam

Desert Storm

Iraq and Pakistan

Worth

Worthy

Work ethic

Writing

Verbal

Virtue

Just a few examples. Begin now to write your own list.

Common phrases that may be helpful:

America, love it or leave it…

…the American way…

...entitled to his/her opinion

Friendship in life is...

I am so sorry. Can you ever forgive me?

I forgive you...

I will share with you a memorable/meaningful lesson in my life...

Giving to charities indicates...

...to lay down one's life...

Make the world a better place...

My greatest/fondest expectations

My strongest commitment is to...

Our family history shows that...

Pay yourself first

Plan your work and work your plan

Skeletons in the closet

Someday I will...

Something for nothing

Take-charge personality

To thine own self be true

Trip to the woodshed with Dad

Your spending habits reflect your values...

Way with words

Lists to work on:

List of family members who should receive my ethical will

List of other people who should get some other version of my ethical will

List of relatives or friends to check dates and details with

Questions to think over:

What bits of wisdom should I bestow on the future generations?

What intangible assets and qualities have I developed in a lifetime?

What place do insight, courage, principles, prayer, perceptions, and values have in my personal philosophy of life?

Which of those will I leave to my loved ones in my legacy letter, or ethical will?

Should I let them in on the secret of my success?

Should I try to outline how they should spend or invest

"my" money when they receive it?

Is it fair to give guidelines for spending?

Should I shock them by telling them the truth about wealth, or let them find their real happiness in their own way?

Has my use and spending of my money reflected my values? my philosophy?

Shall I tell them my view of things--the way it is now and the way I see things?

How can I prepare myself so as not to get my feelings hurt if one of my "heirs" says it is a silly undertaking?

Am I capable of reading aloud the words to tell those close to me that I love them?

How do I tell them of my respect for them?

I have made so many mistakes; how do I begin to explain myself and then ask forgiveness?

How do I explain friendship, especially the kind that goes back to our childhood?

What has our friendship meant to me all through these years?

I can explain how I selected the charities I support, based on their records and successes.

Appendix Three

Ethical Will Resources

Websites and E-mail addresses:

Professional writing assistance:
Association of Personal Historians
Website: www.personalhistorians.org

Ethical Wills:

Website: www.ethicalwillexamples.com
E-mail: foltz@ethicalwillexamples.com

Website: www.ethicalwills.com
E-mail: info@ethicalwill.com

Printers:

The Copy Shop

Copies Unlimited

Office Depot

Office Max

Kinko's

Check your telephone book yellow pages for local printers

Self-Publishers and POD's

Infinity Publishing

1094 New DeHaven Street, Suite 100

West Conshohocken, PA 19428-2713

info@infinitypublishing.com

Toll-free (877) BUY-BOOK

Morris Publishing

3212 East Highway 30

P.O. Box 2110

Kearney, NE 68847

Toll-free (800) 650-7888

These are two I have worked with. There are many others. Use keywords such as self-publishers or self-publishing. Ask lots of questions before you sign anything!

Bibliography

Books

Baines, Barry K., MD. (2002). *Ethical wills Putting your values on paper.* Cambridge, MA: Perseus Books Group. www.ethicalwill.com

Foltz, Sharon, EdD, (1999) *Passing your heritage on: A guide to writing your family stories.* Indianola, IA: Rainbow Ridge Publications, www.rainbowridgepublications.com
foltz@iowatelecom.net
http://www.writewithyou.com
follz@ethicalwillexamples.com

Freed, Rachel. *Women's lives, women's legacies: Passing your beliefs and blessings to future generations.* Fairview Press, 2003

Reimer, Jack and Nathaniel Stampfer, *So That Your Values Live On: Ethical Wills and How to Prepare Them.* Jewish Lights Publishing (1991)

Internet Articles

Clark, Roy P. usatoday.com/news/opinion/
editorials/2006-04-10-forum-memoirs_x.htm

Collier, Charles W. see Elbaum, J. (July 2004) entry

Cornwell, Lisa. (2005, July 5). Interest growing in use
of ethical wills. The Intelligencer (Online).
http://wwwphillyburbs.com/whatsnew/html-2

Crenshaw, Kevin H. Ethical Wills: A memory that
keeps on giving http://www.aces.edu/urban/metronews/
vol2no2/ethical.html

Elbaum, Joy. How to write an ethical will. (Online.)
Parenthood.com

Elbaum, Joy. (2004, July.) Ethical wills: Mapping out
your most meaningful legacy. (Online.) Parenthood.com

Family Giving News, (2004, April) Vol. 4, Issue 4.
Ethical wills and donor legacy statements. National
Center for Family Philanthropy. http:/www.NCFP.ORG

Flashman, Robert, Melissa Flashman, Libby Noble,
and Sam Qiuick. (1998, Fall/Winter). Ethical wills:
passing on treasures of the heart. The Forum for
Family and Consumer Issues 3.3 (Online)

http//\www.ces.ncsu.edu/depts/fcs/pub/1998/wills.html

Flora, Carlin. Self-Portrait in a Skewed Mirror.
Psychology Today Magazine, Jan/Feb 2006

Friedman, Scott E. and Dr. Alan G. Weinstein.
Reintroducing the Ethical Will: Expanding the Lawyer's
Toolbox. American Bar Association, GP/Solo Law
Trends & News Estate Planning Vol. 2, No. 1

Harvey, Paul. Paul Harvey writes
www.ojar.com/view_982.htm

Hurme, Sally. See Steele, J. entry

Josaba Ltd., 1998 Ethical Wills--Example
www.ethicalwill.com

McAdams, Dan. See Flora entry

McAulay, Jean, Ethical wills let people transmit life
lessons learned. www.ajc,com/news, April 23, 2006

McMillen, Tom. (2002, Aug/Sept). Ethical wills
Passing on your values, not just your valuables.
LifeWise Magazine. (Online.)

Morphew, Clark. (1999, March). Bequeathing your
beliefs: ethical wills may help leave blessings,

thoughts, and hope. (Online.) www.abcd-caring.org

Murphy , Kate. The Virtues and Values of an Ethical Will It offers spiritiual wealth and helps estate planning. BusinessWeek online, April 2006.

O'Shaughnessy, Lynn. (2005, April 10). Ethical will can provide a sense of completion. (Online.) http://signonsandiego.com/news/business/shaughness sy/ 20050410-9999-1b10lynn.html

Owen-Toole, Rev. Thomas. (2005, July 14). Ethical wills from generation to generation: Passing along the good life to your children. (Online.) www.uua.org/families/

Perks, Bob. Where there's a will. (Online.) beliefnet.com

Rehl, Kathleen M. PhD, CFP, (2003). Help your clients preserve values, tell life stories and share the "voice of their hearts" through ethical wills. Journal of Practical Estate Planning. (Online.) www.tax.cchgroup.com or rehlmoney@earthlink.net

Robb Report, for the luxury lifestyle. Family: Ethical will power

Rothman, Jonathan. Everyone should have an ethical will. (Online.) http://www.jewishsf.com//content/2/ module/displaystory/story_id/26104/format/html/display story.html

Rubin, David. See Flora entry

Schulman, Miriam (1996, Vol.7, No. 3). A testament to ethics. Markkula Center for Applied Ethics (Online.)

Scott, Betsy. Leaving a legacy. News-Herald.com April 19, 2006

Steele, Jeffrey. Bequeathing values rather than valuables. (Online.) AARP as quoted in latimes.com

Teicher, Stacy A. (2004, July 7). A fresh definition of inheritance comes into vogue. (Online.) http://www.csmonitor.com/200 4/0707/p11s02-lifp.h

Winner, Lara, M.A. Metapsychology, (2002, Jul 9). Mental Help Net's Bookstore (Online)

Ward, Greg. See McAulay entry

Make a joke
    play on words –
" "Waste not want not"
Mother – limericks –
            dictionary –
            games –

Caretaker - in my home - 24/7

Suicide - Martha - Myra - Pat etc.

Confidence

Student

Thrift

Lend a hand

Share -

Popular -

Friendly

Communicate

Tell others they are appreciated

Be interested / interesting

What gives you pride?

" are you ashamed of?

What do you miss? People Activities

Songs - Poems - Nursery Rhymes - Pooh -

Major Events - Depression - WWII - College - Women's roles -

Mentors - Ruthanne - Parents -

Sacrifice -

Values

Beliefs

Principles.

Freedom -

Choice

Attitude

Life choices

Marriage

Education

Cars - new -

see the country - USA

Ability to laugh

to smile

Celebrate holidays -

Traditions - Xmas egg nog -

Nature - Outdoors -

Plants animals Bugs

Flowers - Trees -

Travel - all states

MEX - CANADA

NOVA-SCOTIA -

Child - "Lois" friend

? Friends - ! neighbor

Cheerful - Optomistic

Neighbors -

Rues -

Diversity

Didn't ask? -

Go with flow -

Many years in Health & Wellness -

Medical field -

Social worker ♡

Education - teacher -

learning -

CPSIA information can be obtained
at www.ICGtesting.com
Printed in the USA
LVOW04s1427231215

467646LV00014B/115/P

9 780741 437952